AN AMERICAN BORN IN IRAQ

by

STEVE A. RAHAWI

 WORLD NOVELS

April 18, 2015

To SANDRA

P.O. Box 241852
Los Angeles, California 90024

i

"AN AMERICAN ... BORN IN IRAQ"

P.O. Box 241852
Los Angeles, CA 90024
Tel: (310) 477-5344 • Fax: (310) 477-5055

Processed in the United States of America
ISBN: 978-0-9652565-3-7

8th Printing - December 2013

To purchase a copy or copies of this book,
Contact your favorite bookstore or as bellow

World Novels Distributing Company
P.O. Box 241852, Los Angeles, CA 90024
Tel: (310) 477-5344 • Fax: (310) 477-5055

TABLE OF CONTENTS
"An American... Born in Iraq"

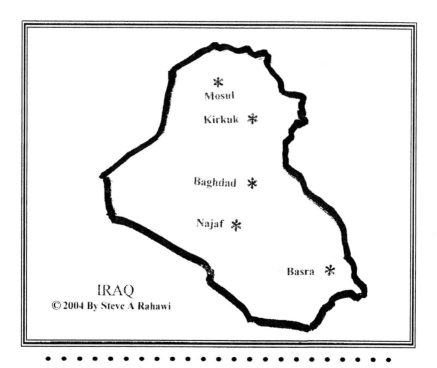

IRAQ
© 2004 By Steve A Rahawi

**My bitter/sweet…long, long journey
From Mosul, Iraq to Los Angeles, California**

Mainland
The United States of America
© 2004 By Steve A. Rahawi

1

My Birth in Iraq and Early Years

Shortly after 11:00 p.m. on Wednesday, September 11, 2002... I sat alone in my small apartment in Westwood, a community in the Western part of Los Angeles, California.

I was in a quiet sadness, with tears welling in my eyes... pondering... how can I show my love for my country, my country that I love... the United States of America?

How can I, an unknown docudramatic writer, express my everlasting gratitude to God and to America... the Land of the Free and the Home of the Brave?

Then suddenly I recalled that three days earlier a good friend of mine for almost 19 years, a kind Los Angeles father of eight sons, by the name of Jonathan E. Johnson, asked me for the third time in two months,

"Steve, have you written your autobiography in two or three pages yet?"

I also recalled my answer to Jonathan (who is my attorney),

"No, I have not yet, but I will."

Thus, about 20 minutes later, I started writing my life story. I wrote two pages, then three pages, and I kept writing, way past midnight.

My fellow Americans, my name is Steve Rahawi... formerly Ahmad Rahawi. I am an American who was born in Iraq, and lived in Iraq for about 18 years. I was born to Moslem parents, but became a Christian about 18 years after I arrived in America.

My fellow Americans, I believe I have a story worthy of sharing with you, and other people around the world, especially at this critical time in the course of current and future American relations with Iraq.

In the city of Mosul, on the Western bank of the fast moving Tigris River in Northern Iraq... on a rainy and gloomy day in the early hours of November 25, 1926, a beautiful and rather small 28 year old Iraqi woman gave birth to a screaming boy.

Moments later, the attending midwife said in Arabic,

"Thank Allah. He is a healthy boy."

Moments later, the perspiring mother said in Arabic,

"Let us name him Ahmad. He is a gift from above."

Thus, I, Steve A. Rahawi, was born into this wonderful wide world. And while it is a great privilege, to almost any Moslem, to be named Ahmad, I elected, when I became a U.S. citizen in 1956, to be officially named Steve A. Rahawi. I really like both names... but "Steve" is my real and legal name.

At the time of my birth, Iraq was a recently independent Arabic-speaking country, with a population of about 5 million (96% Moslem, 3% Christian and 1% Jewish).

However, the Moslem majority actually included many thousands who were descendants of the Ten Tribes of Israel as expounded in the Old Testament. These ten tribes were removed, as captives, by the King of Assyria, from their homeland of Northern Palestine (now Israel) to huge camps near Nineveh... the great capital city of the Assyrian empire.

Both of my parents, and their parents, and grandparents (and on for almost 2800 years), were descendants of the Tribe of Dan, one of the ten tribes of Israel. I believe those Israelites who remained in and around Nineveh (whose ruins are found in the Hills across the Tigris River from Mosul) chose to become Moslems for safety and economic gain.

My father, Abdul-Aziz Rahawi, at the time

of my birth, was a handsome 30 year old. He was stocky built (about 5'7").

He was the older of two sons of a widow, whose husband (my grandfather), died of a broken neck after falling from a suddenly frightened horse. My father was about three years old and his younger brother a few months old, when my grandfather died... leaving my grandmother a poor struggling widow, who never remarried.

My father was illiterate, but gifted with high intelligence and a sharp mind, particularly in business matters. At my birth, he was a struggling self-employed tobacco merchant, who bought from the Kurdish tobacco growers in and around the Kurdish towns of Dahuk and Rawanduz. He then sold what he purchased, at profit, to the tobacco agents for the tobacco factories in Baghdad (Iraq's capital and largest city), and Allepo in Syria.

Though born a Moslem, my father was not serious about Islam. He had as many Christian friends as Moslems, and later on, when he became a very prosperous merchant, two of his most important employees were very devout Christian men. He also loved to chain smoke, and to ride his favorite Arabian horse as often as he could.

But above all, he honored and loved his widowed mother. And my mother never was jealous of that, because she too did truly honor and love her mother-in-law.

However, my father at the age of 29, took on another responsibility. He married a second wife (Moslem men in Iraq at that time were legally allowed to have up to four wives... living in the same place if desired). My father loved my mother and she loved him, but because she did not conceive any child for two years of marriage, he thought she was barren. So he took a pretty Kurdish woman as his second wife. She was a fair looking and easy going, unassuming young woman. Within ten months she delivered a very beautiful blonde headed girl, who was named "Aziza"... meaning very dear. Indeed, Aziza became a very dear person to almost all who knew her. She was my favorite sibling over the years.

About 20 months after Aziza's birth, I was born to my parents and became the first born son to my father... the one son to be prepared to carry on if my father died or became disabled.

Three months after my birth, my father's second wife delivered a son, her first son. They named him Mohammad. He became a jealous younger brother... but generally he was not any threat to me. Fifteen years after his birth he was about three inches taller than me and about 30 pounds heavier. But he never won a running race or a game of marbles with me.

Two years after my birth, the second wife gave birth to Adeeba, and five years later, my mother gave birth to my brother "Thamir", her last child. But the second wife gave my father two more sons, Adeeb (polite) and Ghanim, who was one of the happiest little boys in our neighborhood and in his school.

My mother, Hayat Killah, was the only daughter of a well-to-do sheep and tobacco trader. She loved gold and silver bracelets, rings and earrings... as many as she could get from her father and her husband as well. She really did look very regal with her ornaments, fair face and beautiful smile. She had black hair and brown eyes, and she looked Jewish to many people.

My dear mother was also illiterate as her parents. However, she had a remarkable ability to memorize whatever she heard and a marvelous gift of wisdom... especially when delegating her cooking and household chores to others... except me, because she wanted me to be the top in my class - always.

My mother was also a very effective business advisor to my father. She literally moved him to rise to become one of the most successful tobacco wholesalers, as well as the most successful general cigarette distributor in Mosul (at that time the second largest city in Iraq with a population around 250,000, while Baghdad had about 650,000 inhabitants).

The City of Mosul which had the highest percentage of the Christian population in Iraq (estimated at 8%), also was the third source of Iraq's National Gross Income (after Baghdad and Kirkuk). Kirkuk was a poor provincial center in Northeastern Iraq until the very best oil potential of Kirkuk was discovered and exploited. Thus, the quality of Iraqi oil and its reserves (third in the world, after Saudi Arabia and the Russian Federation), became a great blessing to Iraq.

However, with increasing oil production (and huge financial rewards), Iraq also became increasingly, a seeker of the elusive title of Liberator of the Arab nations. Liberator from what? This somewhat unhealthy attitude, which started back when I was a teenager, has unfortunately (under the excessive ambition of Saddam Hussein) led to the Iraq-Iran

War, the invasion of Kuwait by Iraq, the sanctions and U.N. Resolutions (thus far defied by Saddam Hussein's government)... and to the current crisis. Truly, too much ambition, at the expense of others, is the proven downfall of nations... and human beings, worldwide.

By the time I was about ten, my father had become a prosperous businessman. So he designed and built an unusual house. I have never seen another so unique, either in person or in a photograph. It was great and awful too.

It was built on about half an acre of land in a suburb, which was filled with foreign consulates, professionals and businessmen, as well as poverty stricken households. Outwardly, it was Arabic and Moorish, but like a castle with a wall about 86 feet high. With full respect to my father's many talents, I would never use him as my architect. The entire structure was "Un-American"... it would never quality for any building permit... not even in Malibu (except for its beautiful gardens).

It had a flower and rose garden, with well kept shrubbery and flower beds. It also had a large plot, the center of which was the "take it easy and enjoy" lawn, surrounded by pebble-bottomed ditches with running water, then a grassy walkway surrounded by three foot high, well kept shrubbery on each side. The entire South side of the property was blessed with overhanging grape vines, orange and lemon trees. So you could pick delicious grapes and inviting oranges as you wished, take a reclining cloth lawn chair and relax, converse, and eat. Both gardens were enjoyed throughout the summer in the late afternoons and evenings by many people, besides our own household.

The huge house itself had five levels: the lower basement for food storage to feed a household of 15 persons for a year. Above it was the upper basement, all marble, for summer dining and afternoon siestas. (The siestas were mandatory on all of us kids, between 1:00 and 4:00 p.m. during the hot summer days.) Next was the main floor (a 1,000 square foot marble floor) adjoined by the lavishly furnished visitor's room, the children's study or play room (not much studying was done except when a parent snooped), the maid's room, the wood and fuel storage room, the only bathroom (which almost melted our bones because of its excessive steam), as well as the two sectioned old-fashioned medieval kitchen, and finally the inner gate.

The fourth level of the house contained a wing for my mother and her two children, the second wife and her five children, grandma's large room with its extra nice bed for the day's best behaved boy or girl (with a nice purse of goodies), my father's large suite... then the only restroom... which had a standing line most of the time.

The fifth level was the flat roof. We reached it through a winding staircase from the fourth floor. That roof was a lifesaver from June 15 to September 15 each summer when the evening temperature ranged between 80-90 degrees every night... until it cooled off a few degrees from about 1:00 a.m. to 6:00 a.m. My dad, his mother and wives slept on high four-legged beds. The rest of us slept on mats on the floor... where we often enjoyed the company of a variety of summer insects including ants, spiders, cute little scorpions, and small yellowish centipedes. The roof, of course, was protected by a six foot high extension of the outer wall of the building and an iron guard rail about four feet high to protect an unwary sleepwalker from plunging 80 feet to the marble on the main floor. Quite a place it was.

Meanwhile, over the following ten years,

my father became a prominent businessman socially and in Mosul's Chamber of Commerce as well. His place of business became the gathering place, six days a week - except Fridays - of prominent business leaders, city government officials, and the city judge... as well as hundreds of daily customers who seemed unable to live without cigarettes or chewing tobacco. Indeed, my father's carriage, which he rode in from the house to work and back, became something many people wanted to run along with to request a special favor... or free cigarettes. My father was also very generous at the end of each month of Ramadan, the fast month of the Moslem world. He gave freely to anyone who came to take what they needed or wanted of the meat of sacrificed rams. No female sheep was killed or sacrificed with my father's knowledge.

Speaking of sacrifice, I now remember my own very embarrassing and painful experience when I was circumsized at the age of ten years, older than most Moslem boys. My father decided that it was about time that my brother and I, and two sons of his second wife, be circumsized. We boys had no freedom of choice in the matter. We had to endure it.

When the appointed day came, we boys

were circumsized, with no enthusiasm, right in the presence of about 200 men and boys, and about 400 women and girls (men and women were separated of course). And as each son collapsed in pain or fear, or both... when the foreskin was cut off by a special, razor sharp knife... there arose a great hollering (and the special Arabic tongue music) from the completely packed main floor of the house and the two levels above it. And what is more, we boys were expected to show how courageous we were by smiling broadly, as we were carried to our respective beds on the fourth floor... being taunted by giggling young girls and being kissed by many pious Moslem grandmothers who looked upon us as Angels of God... that day only of course.

However, as I look back on my years of childhood and young years in Mosul, Iraq, my memory flashes back to many activities, events and experiences that are worthy of sharing with my children and grandchildren, and I feel perhaps of some interest to you, the reader.

My earliest recollection of my childhood on this wonderful planet is when I was about three years old. I clearly remember being held very lovingly and carefully by my father as I rode in front of him on his saddled white Arabian horse. We were taking a leisurely ride, about a mile or so from the outskirts of the city, galloping softly once in a while... to my great delight and my encouragement to my father to do it some more.

My second vivid recollection is that of myself sitting on a bench with my mother, surrounded by a garden in a hospital in Baghdad, the capital of Iraq. I was in the process of recovering from an operation on my neck for my thyroid gland or goiter. I was about five years old and my mother was nursing me patiently.

Another experience I remember (at the age of seven or eight), is that of my mother, myself and my grandmother (then about 65 years old) resting on a hot summer day in a room on the first floor of an old house in a medieval part of Mosul. This was before my father became a rich man.

Suddenly, a huge snake (about five feet in length and two inches in diameter), emerged from a hole in the corner of the room. I was terrified, but my mother, a woman of courage in time of crisis, got up, looked at the snake and said calmly (in Arabic of course), "You big snake, listen to me. You share this house with us, so don't you bother us, and we won't bother you." In an instant, the snake stretched its body to its full length, as if on parade, and crept into another hole in another corner of the room. We never saw that snake again for the full year or so afterwards that we remained in that house.

There was also the time, when I was about nine years old, that I became a ruthless marble player... not only in our neighborhood but of my entire elementary school of 500 boys.

I became so skilled and sharp-eyed at shooting marbles (1" to 1 1/2" in diameter), that I literally cleaned up over 30 boys from age eight to eleven years old. I became rich in marbles. Then I did the same thing with boys from my school who accepted my challenge. I won over 300 marbles, and I started selling them back... until my father stopped me.

Another memorable experience happened when I was about thirteen. My father wanted my half brother (Mohammad) and me to learn to swim in the Tigris River (a fast moving, half-mile wide river at the time). We walked eight miles every day that entire summer to meet (along with four other boys about our age) our swimming instructor, who had his office on a coffee shop bench at the edge of the river. About 200 feet South of the huge bridge that crossed the Tigris River, our instructor taught us to swim.

During the first few days, each of us six boys were fastened to an inflated goat skin. Mine was the smallest, and I did not float well. I was not swimming as well as my half brother. For several weeks he kept bragging at home and among our neighborhood friends that he could swim twice as fast as I could. Finally, one afternoon, when our swimming instructor excused himself for a cup of coffee with a friend on the farthest bench of the coffee shop, Mohammad started bragging again. By then, all of us in the swimming class were able to swim without the inflated goat skins. Suddenly I became so angry with Mohammad, that I told my bragging half brother, "Okay, I dare you to race me... under water!" He quickly replied, almost shouting, so the other four boys could hear him, "Let us do it right now!"

Then, in two seconds, he dived into the fast current... and I followed instantly. After awhile, I felt out of breath with my lungs ready to explode, but I wanted to win the race so badly. A little later (which felt like a terrible dream), I began to black out... but I could not surface.

Moments later (I was told), our instructor heard the other four boys screaming in alarm, and upon learning of the race, he dove in after us. Luckily he found me and pulled me out of the swift current, about 100 feet south of my starting point. He then began breathing into my mouth and applying hand pressure to my stomach.

About a minute later (as I was told), I vomited a lot of water and slowly began to breath. As I opened my eyes, I felt like I was awaking from a terrible dream. I saw my half brother, Mohammad, weeping in relief... and perhaps happiness too.

By the way, I did win that race because Mohammad surfaced from swimming under water about fifty feet from the spot where I was snatched from being drowned.

At about 15 1/2 years old, I had another frightening experience involving one of my classmates, the horse-loving son of the Commander of the Northern Cavalry Division of the Iraqi Army. This division consisted of several thousand men, horses, and mules whose purpose was to suppress the Kurds in Northern Iraq, who often rebelled against Baghdad.

In a once-in-a-lifetime opportunity, my

friend's father authorized his son to invite me to participate in a six week summer course... to become a skilled horseman, on the huge army horses. The other eleven participants were 14-16 year old boys who were sons of cavalry officers.

I was reluctant to accept the offer, but my father encouraged me to do so.

During our first meeting, the trainer explained (in plain Arabic) the several challenging horse riding tricks he was going to teach us. As he finished talking, I knew that I was destined to be kicked out in a couple of days... for hopeless performance.

However, I managed to perform almost as well as the other boys. But, one drill was very forbidding to me.

By sheer good luck, on the final day when each of us competed in two events, I won the event that was most difficult for me. To my great surprise, I actually won that event... standing in crossed-over stirrups and saluting while the horse was galloping.

The following morning, each of the twelve of us stood by our assigned huge army horse, to receive at least one medal.

Then minutes later, at the very moment my name was called for me to accept my automatic medal for not missing any training session, and the one for winning as Best Rider (for my most feared event), the unthinkable happened... my horse suddenly lifted his huge and powerful left front hoof (intentionally or not, I could not tell and still don't know) and slammed it unto my left foot, right over my left big toe. An unbelievable pain and shock went through my entire body and mind. But, under the circumstances, I simply could not faint. I actually managed to receive both medals with a smile and a word of thanks, in the presence of the only army horse I have ever had the privilege of scrubbing, watering and riding.

A few minutes later, with my left sock and boot in a bloody mess, I was driven to the office of Dr. Yahya, our family physician (a cousin of my father...their mothers being sisters), whose European style home joined ours.

The medals? I gave one to my full brother, Thamir, and the other I kept.

There is one very important thing I have not mentioned concerning my father. When I was 14, my father and our neighbor across the street (who was almost a non-practicing Moslem... like my father), went together on an extended business trip to Damascus, Syria.

About a month later they returned, each accompanied by a new 24 year old wife. My father's third wife was 20 years younger than my father. Within a week, all three of my father's wives were making adjustments. These adjustments included my father's new wife calling his suite... hers.

Within six years after marrying his third wife, my father had three sons and a very smart daughter named Mona, by his third wife. Thus, my father became the father of 11 children... from his three wives.

2

My Elementary and Junior High School Years in Iraq

In 1932, when I was almost six years old, the City of Mosul, Iraq's second largest city, had nine elementary schools and three junior high schools for boys. It also had four elementary schools and two junior high schools for girls.

Elementary schools were for first through eighth grades, and junior high schools were for 9th and 10th grades. There was mandatory schooling for boys through the 8th grade, except for blind, deaf or retarded boys. Schooling was not mandatory for girls. There were no kindergartens for boys or girls.

In September of 1932, I was enrolled in first grade in the closest elementary school to our house. Even though I was shy of being six years old by 80 days, I was admitted because (according to my father, my mother and the father of one of my best neighborhood pals), I was very smart. And my mother quickly saw to it that I became the brightest pupil in my class... which included my being on time always (in spite of the creek bed on our walking path to school which became an impassable torrent many days in the winter which required us to walk to school following a much longer route).

Our school, like all the others in the system, started the school day with all the students and teachers standing in orderly rows to sing a school song honoring our country. Then we ended our song with a salute to the flag of Iraq with the right hand (or the left it you were left handed). We then separated to classes quietly. Yes, quietly, because we had to, or else the guilty boy would have to stand silently in the corner of the room by the blackboard for 10 minutes.

I was always acting properly, and my teachers bragged about me to the other teachers and to the school principal... who in turn reported this good behavior to my parents, through notes he gave to me to deliver to them. My little fruit box which I took to school almost always had more fruit than I could eat. So I sold the surplus fruit to the neighborhood kids in exchange for colored marbles.

During the following five years, I was an ideal elementary school student... through the end of the fifth grade.

But things changed during the sixth grade, which I started as an eleven year old. I became the boy who loved silly jokes and remarks... the sillier and funnier the better.

And sure enough, I became best friends with another boy in my class... who was just as joke loving as I was. We literally kept our class laughing and joking half the time. We had two teachers who taught us all the subjects. One was a red-headed bespectacled teacher about 25 and the other a mean, older looking man.

Then one morning a month later, after a burst of laughter with my pal, the older, mean looking teacher called me to the front of the class of about 30 students. Each of us had his wooden desk with its attached flat top.

I stood in front of the teacher who shouted at me "Attention!" I did, like a rigid Nazi German soldier. Then he shouted at me, "At ease."

And I did relax and looked at my funny pal with the corner of my eye, who started making funny gestures with his hands, which in turn made me start to smile (because I could not help it). Then, instantly, my teacher slapped my face, in an intense burst of anger, so hard that I was actually thrown several feet away to the floor.

He ordered me to sit quietly. And it worked. The whole class became silent as a cemetery in winter.

When I got home, my face and left eye were swollen, and my parents wanted to know what had happened. I did not tell them, nor anyone else in the family. But I was unable to go to school the rest of the week.

The first day of the following week, after the song and flag exercise, the same teacher smiled at me for the first time ever, took me aside, and said to me, "Ahmad, I am sorry I had to slap you so hard. Please forgive me. You are, from this minute forward, my class monitor... to keep the class quiet. Will you help me?"

And he had tears in his eyes as he waited for my answer. I looked at him and felt his sincerity and replied, "Sure. I will do it. I promise, on my Boy Scout honor."

And that teacher, who had seldom smiled and had sounded like a boring history and geography teacher to me... became to me and many other students in the 6th grade classes... a most cheerful teacher with very interesting and inspiring history and geography lessons... which over the years have proved to be of great worth to me.

And I, Ahmad Rahawi, the first Boy Scout in the history of the Rahawi family, did keep my Boy Scout promise.

In early September of 1940, when I was nearly 14 years old, I started the 9th grade in a recently built junior high school in the nicest section of the city. It was about three miles from my house.

When going to and from my new school, I had to cross a large open area, which became a wonderful garden of wild flowers in April and May, but a muddy field in the winter, and a barren desert in the summer.

There were about 800 students (all teen-age boys from three neighboring elementary schools, including the one I attended). So, many knew me and the good and bad of my character... including my reputation as a lover of history and geography, a lover of the five mile race, and a lover of football (which meant soccer in Iraq at that time).

So I studied hard, arriving at school on time, making friends with the 60 Christian students, and the remaining four Jewish students. Over 80% of the Jewish population of Mosul, by then, had left to join Jews arriving in Palestine from all over the Arab world,

voluntarily or because of increasing persecution by the Moslem majority and government
agencies.

In junior high, I began taking English
classes an hour each day, along with my other
seven hours (including a happy hour of History
class and another hour in World Geography
and Cultures). I also took French lessons three
hours a week in the summer of 1941.

In addition to all the above, I also played
soccer in and out of school, ran many miles
weekly, and walked briskly to and from
school.

With so much to do in and out of school,
I stopped reading the Koran to my illiterate
grandmother, father and mother. Instead, I
began reading about other countries and their
histories... especially a far, far away great
land... called the United States of America.

Then in February of 1942, the Ministry of
Education in Baghdad came up with a unique
program... called "King Faisal Pre-Mission
High School" for the top 56 male students in
Iraq. The program would accept only four stu-
dents from each of the 14 provinces in Iraq.

These selected students were to live in
government financed dormitories and attend
classes in Baghdad for two academic years.

Furthermore, following two years of study, with a heavy dose of daily English and practice... the very, very fortunate students would be sent to a university in England or to the American University in Beirut, Lebanon.

That announcement to 10th graders in all Iraq meant something very special to me. I began preparing, with my mother's increasing support, to become among the lucky four to be chosen from the province of Mosul... subject to national competitive tests, starting on June 3, 1942.

Finally came the big week, the first week of June 1942, when all 10th graders in the entire country of Iraq assembled in courtyards of every junior high school in the country, to take a series of tests over five days from 9:00 a.m. to 12:00 noon daily.

As I sat at my assigned wooden desk with its attached flat top, I was sufficiently calm that I could smile to one of the officials whom I recognized as one of my former teachers in elementary school (the redheaded one).

Then at 9:00 a.m. sharp, the questions and required essay of the day were read aloud (no microphone at that time). Then each student received a printed copy of the test... all in

Arabic of course.

How happy I was. The questions on the first day were perfect for me. They concentrated on Arab civilization and culture, and a required essay on the Arab (the Moors) rule in Spain. I was smiling in my seat because this was what I was dreaming about, the realm of my great love: History.

I wrote that morning with unrestrained feelings and admiration for all the contributions that the Arabs have contributed to the world... under Haroon Rasheed (the famous Kalif in Baghdad in the Middle Ages)... as well as the Arabs in Spain. And it was from my heart, because the truth is easy to praise and testify of... always.

The following day and fifth day also brought tests that I answered with knowledge and zeal.

About 60 days later, I was officially advised by the principal of my junior high school and notified by an official letter, that I was chosen by the Ministry of Education in Baghdad to be one of the four students from the Province of Mosul to attend King Faisal Special High School in Baghdad... as one of the 56 chosen nationwide, based on my final average for all subjects of the junior high school national

5-day examination. I also learned from the same sheet, attached to the letter I received, that I was the only student in Mosul Province to score 100 out of a possible 100 on all three subjects (related to History and Geography) without which I could not have been selected. (Sometimes it is good to be slapped in the face.)

Interestingly, two of the other three selected with me from Mosul Province were Christians. One was the son of a Christian bookkeeper. The other was a very unsophisticated 16 year old from an Assyrian town North of Mosul. Both of them became my friends during our two years at King Faisal Special High School.

3

My Four Years in Baghdad and Beirut

After a million kisses from my family and family friends, at home and at the Mosul Railway Station, I boarded the train on the afternoon of September 2, 1942, to begin classes at King Faisal Special High School... in Baghdad.

It was the first time in my life to travel in a car, on a bus or on a train... alone.

The train was jam packed. Some passengers were actually standing and holding on to the steel columns in the aisles. And every time the train made a stop from its 25 mile per hour Southern course on the way to Baghdad... it stopped with a jar that sent those passengers who were standing, reeling back and forth.

As night fell upon us, a dim light replaced the sunlight, and a Kurdish girl (about 17 or 18) purposely or otherwise, almost sat on my lap. I was uncomfortable with the strange feelings I felt every time this girl's face almost touched my face. So I got up and stood almost twelve hours, until the train arrived at Baghdad's train station, which seemed at least three times larger than the one at Mosul.

I was met at the train station by a Lebanese national, named Fareed, about 30, who was the Assistant to the General Manager (Mr. Tabbarah) of the largest cigarette factory in Baghdad and all of Iraq... whom my father represented in Mosul as a General Distributor. Mr. Tabbarah was also Lebanese. Fareed took me to the elegant guest house for the factory where Fareed had his living quarters.

That night I stayed at this lovely home and discovered that it had the first bathroom that I had ever seen... with a shower. I stood under that shower for almost 20 minutes, alternating hot and cold water, until I accidentally turned the hot water knob a little too hot and literally jumped through the shower curtain to barely escape the scalding water.

About half an hour later, I was sitting on a heavily padded arm chair... and there was a beautiful silver tray full of cigarettes next to the padded arm chair. I had never tried to smoke a cigarette in my life before, even though I had many opportunities to do so, both at home and at my father's tobacco warehouse and cigarette sales center.

I don't know what got into me, but I took one of the cigarettes, lighted a match to it, and put the cigarette to my lips... inhaled once... deeply.

Suddenly, I had a truly terrible feeling in my mouth and in my lungs, and I started coughing so hard that Fareed came running over to me wondering why I was coughing so hard. When I told him what happened, he looked at me, smiled and said, "Ahmad, I don't think you are going to enjoy being a partner or an heir in your father's business."

Then he added, laughing, "Unless you want to give it another try."

Still teary eyed from coughing, I answered, "I am sure I will never have another cigarette in my mouth as long as I live." And until this day, almost 60 years from that evening, I have never had, and I never will have any cigarette or tobacco product on my lips or in my mouth.

Later that evening, Fareed took me to dinner at a restaurant at the Hotel Babylon in Baghdad, only a block from the longest bridge straddling the Tigris River. There he told me about his 18 months in America, visiting one of his American Lebanese relatives.

I was completely fascinated by what he told me. And from that evening on, I felt a deep desire to come to America... some day in the future.

The next day, Fareed took me to register at King Faisal High School, located about two miles from the cigarette factory. There we met the two Christian students from Mosul and several British as well as Egyptian instructors, who were graduates of British universities.

Equally important, I learned that very first day that the 56 male students, including myself (four from each of the 14 provinces of Iraq), were to be taught British etiquette and good manners... in order to prepare us to represent Iraq as a well mannered nation.

Thus for the next two years I spent nine months each year in Baghdad, returning to Mosul only for the three month summer vacation.

At King Faisal High School, I mingled day and night with the other students from the other thirteen provinces of Iraq, a country the size of California. Half of the students were from the Shiite division of Islam, and generally they were darker skinned and more studious than the Sunni Moslems of Northern Iraq.

School wasn't all studies; we 56 students

also had a great time playing football (called soccer in America). I played center half because I was faster and smaller in size than most of the players. We also played hooky on Saturdays. My Christian fellow students and I became experts on the great 12 mile long Rasheed Street.

Our British teachers included one from Cambridge University who became my favorite instructor, despite the fact that math was a subject that least interested me. Another instructor was an Oxford University graduate who was in charge of dining room discipline, as well as inspector of the dorms. He taught Geometry and Elementary Physics, and I disliked both. He almost flunked me, except he was very impressed by how neat and clean I kept my bed and my part of the dorm. A month later, he made me night inspector for my dorm.

Then, one day just about a month from graduation, I and my Christian friend from Mosul had an honest conversation about what we really wanted to do after graduation. He wanted to go as a student to the United States... as I did.

However, two months later, when our foreign mission locations were given to us, he was sent to England and I was assigned to "The American University in Beirut ("AUB").

Thus, when I was about 18, I enrolled as a Freshman at the American University in Beirut, Lebanon. This was the first time in my life that I had ever been to any country... other than Iraq... and my father was against it.

"AUB" at that time was a four year accredited university with about 80 faculty members, headed by a tall, slender, bespectacled man. We addressed him, with reverence "President Dodge". He was the first and one of the most disciplined Americans I have ever met. And again, I was very much impressed.

At "AUB" every morning, six days a week, the student body of almost 1,800 students (mostly from Arab countries, including two dozen from Iraq), met in the Assembly Hall to sing "Far far away, beyond the waters, lies the campus of the college... where we love to be...". At the time, there were about 400 students from what is now Israel.

At "AUB" I acquired many experiences. I witnessed, first hand, the hatred that Israeli students had toward the approximately 200 Palestinian and Jordanian students and vice versa. There were many verbal clashes daily...

and sometimes a fist fight. I had no part in any of it.

Not into making straight "A" grades, I was very busy, truthfully, dancing, having dates and having a good time. I also enjoyed swimming at the "AUB" beach... until one day my foot was caught by a small octopus. Reacting, I slipped and injured my knee and was unable to dance, or run to catch the tram (which ran on Rue Bliss adjacent to the campus) to downtown Beirut... the entertainment capital of the Middle East.

After recovering from my knee injury, I spent a month of the following summer completing my second year at "AUB"... but also enjoying with another student from Iraq, the Cedars of Lebanon, the great trees from which the ancient temple of Solomon was primarily built.

While Beirut is the entertainment capital of the Middle East... now... as it was when I was a student at "AUB", one of my greatest memories of Lebanon was the thrill of swimming in the Mediterranean, on a very warm day in July 1946, and then hiking six hours up the mountains to the small village of Biscantah.

My fellow student from Iraq and I could not afford a hotel room, so we lodged with a Christian Lebanese family and I fell in love with their very charming 22 year old daughter. But alas, after a week I ran out of money, and had to sell my camera and my new watch in order to get a ticket on an old bus that went all the way from Beirut to Baghdad (a distance of about 600 miles).

The bus went clinking along, with about 40 passengers, at an average speed of 30 miles an hour, crossing the bone dry Syrian Desert, then following, for over 200 miles, the Euphrates River (from Anah in Western Iraq to Al Ramadi), and then due East, about 50 miles of flat land, to Baghdad.

In Baghdad, I met with Mr. Wood, Principal of King Faisal High School, who was an Englishman from London but the son of a Hindu mother.

Mr. Wood (about 60 years old) and I (nearly 20 years old) had a nice chat in his office. When he asked me what my plans were for the future, I replied, "I really hope for higher education in an American university." I then added, "However, since my father expects me as his eldest son to help him run the family tobacco business, he would never approve of my future study in America... and since I know no one in America and none of my relatives has ever been to America, I can only dream and hope."

Mr. Wood took off his glasses, put them on his desk, then... looking straight at the ceiling, seemed in a deep trance for almost a minute. Then he put his glasses back on, and started digging through the files in front of him on his large desk.

He then said to me, "Ahmad, I am going to write a summary of your school record during your two years here." Then he did write, in his excellent handwriting and with his ink fountain pen, a special letter of recommendation. He looked at me with a fatherly smile and said, "And I am going to add to this letter that you were a very good center half in all the seven football games you played in your second year." And he did so write, to my happy surprise.

That was the last time I saw Mr. Wood, a very special principal for a very special high school in Baghdad, Iraq... King Faisal High School.

That afternoon, I met with my friend Fareed, still the Assistant to the General Manager of the tobacco factory which my father continued to represent as General Distributor in Mosul.

As we got in his car, he turned to me and said, with typical encouragement, "Ahmad, when you get to America, and I believe somehow, you are going to be admitted to an American university... work hard and smile a lot. Make good grades so you can have permission to work part-time by the U.S. Immigration office."

Then he patted me on my shoulder and said, "And don't forget to get yourself a good sweater before your first snow storm in America." And we both laughed.

Twenty minutes later we reached the Baghdad Railway Station. We got out of his car and walked to the ticket counter. He purchased a ticket for me, stuck it in my shirt pocket and said, smiling, "Ahmad, wish me luck. I am moving to Beirut next week. I found the woman of my dreams. Maybe we will meet in America some day. But if we never meet again, remember me with a prayer."

Two minutes later we waived to each other as true friends. That was the last time we met.

4

The Tennis Match that Helped Me Come to America

On the train that hot and muggy day, heading straight North to Mosul, there were over 100 people around me in the train car. Some were dozing, some smoking, some chattering, and even a few were reading the Koran... but I was thinking.

"How can I go to America? And who will finance my trip? And how will I pay for my schooling and living in America?"

I knew that I was no longer qualified for sponsorship by the Ministry of Education in Baghdad, because neither I nor my father had signed the agreement requiring me after university graduation, to work as an employee or contracted professional for the government of Iraq. This would be required if the government were to finance my foreign college education.

Furthermore, my two years as a student at the American University in Beirut were so unorthodox and independent... that my father, as was required by a prior written agreement, had to reimburse the government for my tuition for those two years at "AUB" in Beirut.

Furthermore, I knew that my father was having some health problems, in his lungs, and was facing the growing educational needs of his other ten children, as well as a growing problem with his mentally disabled younger brother.

Thus, for hours on that crowded train, I stood by the door that led to the next car... deep in thought... who would help me go to America? Who would? Who would?

The following day, about noon, my mother and younger full brother "Thamir" welcomed me at the Mosul train station with hugs and kisses. Then the three of us walked the quarter mile to the Rahawi compound (sorry, no taxis in Mosul at that time).

That evening, as our large family (my father, his three wives and eleven children; my grandmother had died when I was in Beirut) sat for dinner, my father somehow never said a single word to me. He knew of my real intentions.

After dinner, my father, mother and brother Thamir and I sat in the shady portion of our large garden. I was enjoying dipping my right hand in the bubbling water which danced over the pebbles in the shallow, one foot diameter ditch, which encircled the garden.

Suddenly, my father said to me, "Ahmad, now that you have had 14 years of schooling... in Mosul, Baghdad and Beirut... and soon you will be 20 years old, isn't it time you started working for pay?"

Surprised at my father's remarks about me working for pay, I replied, rather annoyed, "Dad, aren't you glad that you have a son who can read, write, and speak in Arabic and English?"

Father kept silent for almost two minutes, then said, slowly, "Ahmad... you are my eldest son. You are my natural heir for our family tobacco business. I know you don't like my smoky place of business. I know you want to go to America. But son, I need you at my side. I am not in good health any more. Why don't you start learning to become my junior partner? Will you start tomorrow?"

I kept still for a long minute, then replied, "I will start tomorrow working as a part-time employee, if you accept me at 10 Dinars per day."

My father, mother and Thamir started laughing. Then my father said, "Ten Dinars per day? That is the weekly salary of my book-keeper. You know son, you are in Iraq, not in America. How about five Dinars per day?"

I replied, graciously, "That is half what I asked... but I will accept, provided I work only five hours a day, because I want to improve my tennis game and continue practicing my English at Uncle Yahya's tennis court."

My father, smiling wisely, replied, "Ahmad, you will make a good salesman. I accept your terms."

The next day I rode with my father in his expensive carriage, leaving the house at 7:00 a.m. to his tobacco office and warehouse.

Thus, I kept working at 5 Dinars per day... never having a cigarette in my mouth, but of course inhaling lots of smoke... the "best" smoke in the world though (as my father told his customers, "Because it was the smoke from Khazi, the finest cigarette brand in the world.").

After three months of working at five Dinars per day (plus an additional bonus of 10 Diners, whenever I helped one of the sales representatives or the Kurdish Assistant, Mustafa, close a sale of over 100 Dinars), I had accumulated 700 Dinars. This was equivalent to two years of salary for some municipal government workers in Mosul at the time.

I did not keep my money in the bank. No sir, I entrusted it to a very careful businesswoman, my mother, who kept it in the heavily padded mattress on her two foot high bed, located in the coziest corner of her large bedroom.

Then one morning at about 9:00 a.m. on a beautiful, sunny day in October of 1946, I was alone practicing my lethal serve on the tennis court belonging to my father's cousin, Dr. Yahya. His house was separated from our house by a seven foot wall.

On that day, this large European styled house belonging to Dr. Yahya, was rented by the British Consulate in Mosul, because Dr. Yahya had moved his medical practice to Baghdad. The British Consulate had made the tennis court into a social and sporting hub for the hundred or so Europeans who lived in Mosul, and their guests.

Suddenly, a very cheerful foreign looking woman entered the tennis court from the side door that connected it with the main compound.

Within minutes I learned that her name was "Bismat Theodore" and that she was 34 years old, and a teacher in a small college in the State of Michigan in the United States of America. I also learned that her mother was an Assyrian Christian who was born in Mosul, and her father was a Greek Armenian. She informed me that she had taken a six month leave of absence to spend in Greece and Iraq, particularly in Mosul, and that she was returning to the United States the following week to prepare for her marriage in April. She also told me that she had been invited by an acquaintance at the British Consulate in Mosul to use the tennis court, whenever she wished, but she had been too busy.

Well, here I was, a 20 year old Iraqi chatting with the first American born woman with Iraqi roots that I had ever met in my life. Moreover, I felt so comfortable with Bismat. She was laughing and smiling so freely, as if she had known me for years. During our conversation I told her that I was Ahmad Rahawi, and that I was a lover of America and all that America stood for.

I then said to her, politely and cheerfully, "Miss Theodore, I know you Americans are the best in the world in tennis. How about giving me the most exhausting tennis match in my four years of playing tennis?"

She replied laughing, "How about you

showing me that the handsome Iraqi boys don't mind losing a tennis match... even to a 34 year old woman!"

Then we both laughed again, shook hands, and started a wonderful tennis match... interspersed with jokes. She bested me in that match (or perhaps I helped her beat me): 6-4 and 6-3.

After the match, as we were wiping the sweat from our necks and faces, I looked at her (with tears in my eyes). Bismat was startled and said very kindly, "Ahmad, why the tears?"

Then, humbly and sincerely I said to Bismat, "Can you help me be accepted in an American university or college as a family-supported, not government-supported, foreign student from Iraq?"

She was motionless for almost two minutes, as she stood, her tennis racket in her right hand and her white towel in her left. Then she said to me, touching my shoulder, "Ahmad, I promise to get you accepted by my Alma Mater, Walla Walla College in the State of Washington, where I graduated... or at the University of Denver in Denver, Colorado, where I have good contacts."

An hour later, Bismat Theodore and I shook hands, as she said to me, "You will hear from me in six weeks." Then, she left me with another of her cheerful and easy going American smiles.

True to her promise, Bismat Theodore sent me, in about six weeks, an approved admission from the University of Denver, in Denver, Colorado.

Several weeks later, with a valid passport in hand, scholastic documents, my 700 Dinars (plus another 1000 Dinars from my father, plus some of my mother's gold and silver jewelry which she gave me with a hundred kisses all over my face), I left my father, mother, my ten siblings, and my father's two other wives, and our maid... with tears in each one's eyes... to begin my journey to America.

5

From Alexandria, Egypt, to New York ... by Ship

My train from Mosul arrived in Baghdad early the next morning. Shortly after, I was delivered by carriage for hire, to stay over night at a small but excellent hotel (across the street from the modern Babylon Hotel), where my father often stayed when he came to Baghdad on business trips, or to see me when I was a student at King Faisal High School.

Luckily, the man at the registration desk recognized me, because I had been there several times to meet my father when he came to Baghdad, and to share with him his huge meals. What was luckier for me, was the insistence of the desk clerk that I accept the hospitality of the hotel and occupy the same room where my father usually stayed... free of charge.

A few minutes after insisting that I accept the hotel's hospitality, I accepted the clerk's offer with a handshake, and occupied my father's favorite room overlooking the Tigris

River.

What was even more generous, the hotel insisted that I accept both lunch and dinner free of charge... which I accepted outwardly reluctant, but inwardly welcoming... because I wanted to save all I could for the 10,000 mile trip ahead of me, on my way to my future Alma Mater, the University of Denver.

As I sat for lunch at a small table overlooking the wide Tigris River where it bisects Baghdad into the rich Eastside and the poor Westside, I noticed a tall young man at the next table, looking at me as if he wanted to talk with me. But he did not know how to start a conversation, so I got up and greeted him in Arabic. However, he answered me in Persian and somehow I understood. So I introduced myself in English. He proceeded to get up and spoke to me in surprisingly good English. And with a very slight British accent, he said to me, "My name is Reza and I am from Tehran, the capital of Iran."

Then he politely asked, "Would you like to have lunch with me?"

I replied cheerfully, "Of course." And I proceeded to introduce myself as I began, with his help, to move my large lunch to his table.

He quickly learned that I was on my way to Alexandria, Egypt, then to the United States of America. And very quickly, I also learned that he too was on his way to Alexandria, Egypt... and then on to London, England where his father was an important Iranian businessman who had been separated from his family in Tehran for seven years due to World War II.

Shortly after we finished lunch, Reza and I went a few blocks on Rasheed Street (the longest street in the Middle East) to a British operated bank; he to exchange his money to English Pounds... and I to exchange all my money (except one Dinar) to U.S. Dollars.

We also went about two more blocks to purchase bus tickets (only a few years before had city to city bus service been introduced into Iraq). Our 24 passenger bus was to leave the next morning for Damascus and then on to Jerusalem, and to Cairo, Egypt. Reza paid for his bus fare in English pounds (which was accepted in Iraq at the time by some businesses); and I paid for my fare in U.S. dollars.

That night I could hardly sleep because I was coming down with a sudden chest cold. But I was on time to meet Reza to walk over to the bus station. As we left the hotel, I carried my two suitcases which weighed about 30 pounds each. He carried his two larger and heavier suitcases.

The bus carried 22 other passengers plus the driver who was a large man, who explained profusely the need to have enough food, in the event we had a breakdown and became stranded. Then we began the journey at 30-40 miles per hour, on poor roads most of the time, from Baghdad across Western Iraq.

Meanwhile, my cold had gotten worse, and I began to cough and sneeze. As we crossed the Iraq-Syrian border at about three P. M., I was burning with a fever. Reza, sitting next to me, shared his many interesting stories about Iran and his love for Iranian music and belly dancing girls. He was about 23 years old, and truly a very pleasant young man... who did almost all the talking because my cold was getting worse by the hour.

Finally we arrived in Damascus and had to wait overnight for some needed repairs to our bus.

About 24 minutes after arriving in Damascus, my friend Reza, now exhausted from carrying his two suitcases and the heavier of my two suitcases, checked us into an old hotel near the bus station where we shared the same room.

As we sat for dinner in the hotel's tiny restaurant, I couldn't eat anything. But I did manage to drink some water, with Reza sitting across from me looking sad and bewildered at my condition.

Then, handing me another napkin to blow my swollen nose, he said to me slowly, choking with genuine emotion, "Ahmad, I am a Moslem who believes in Allah, and in helping my friends any time I can."

Then with tears in his dark brown eyes, he said to me, "Allah willing, you and I are going to make it to Cairo... even if I have to carry you on my back."

With my eyes swollen and teary, I thanked him and told him where I kept my passport, my scholastic records, and all my money.

About midnight that night in that paper walled room, Reza helped me change into my pajamas and helped me climb into the high bed.

Neither of us had any kind of medicine with us, and neither of us talked about me going to a doctor or a hospital.

A few minutes later, as I lay on my bed, my head began a journey that I will never forget. In a few moments, as I saw Reza standing by my bed, I passed out unconscious.

The next thing I recognized and heard, was our bus traveling through a street in Jerusalem, and some sounds, and Reza holding me in my seat next to him. Then I passed out again.

The next thing I recognized, when I opened my eyes (with the strangest feeling that I have never experienced again), were vague faces staring at me. They were faces I never had seen before... a man, a woman and two young children all staring at me without a word.

Then the man, dressed as an Egyptian laborer, with long flowing Arab garments and an old European style coat, touched my head gently, lifted it up and gave me some water in a tin cup... which I drank very slowly.

A minute or so later, I sat. Yet my body had absolutely no strength in it. All I could do was look around me slowly. I was in a small room on a thin mattress on the floor with two blankets by my feet.

Slowly I asked in my Iraqi accented Arabic, "Where am I?"

The man answered in Egyptian accented Arabic, "You are in Cairo, Egypt."

Then he added very softly, "I am Ahmad

and this is my wife and my children. Three days ago I was carrying passenger luggage at the bus station in Cairo, when a worried looking man motioned to me to come to him."

Then Ahmad rubbed tears off his cheeks and added slowly, "This man took me inside the bus and I saw you lying there across the bus bench. I thought you were dead and I was afraid to go near you. But the man said to me, "I am Reza from Iran and this is my very sick friend, Ahmad from Iraq."

Then the Egyptian Ahmad told me that Reza had said to him,

"In the name of Allah, I ask you to take care of my very sick friend, in your home, until he gets well... because tomorrow my ship leaves Alexandria to England and I must take that ship."

Ahmad, the Egyptian, continued to tell me, "Your friend gave me your two suitcases and all your money. In the name of Allah, I have not taken anything that belongs to you. It is all here in the corner of this room."

Then he added, "Thanks to Allah, before your friend took the train to Alexandria, he gave me thirty English Pounds to take care of you... Thanks to Allah."

By then, his wife, smiling kindly to me,

came with a metal dish filled with soup and a portion of flat loaf bread. She dipped a small piece of bread into the soup, and with her and her husband holding me up, brought the piece of bread to my mouth, which I ate. They must have spent an hour feeding me very slowly.

Ahmad's peaceful home was made of mud and some wood (the most humble home I had ever slept in), but a home full of the love of God.

Four days later, having regained most of my strength, but looking ten pounds thinner, Ahmad and his wife took me in an old carriage to board a train to Alexandria, Egypt's major seaport on the Mediterranean Sea.

After I purchased my train ticket, I tried to give 30 Dollars to my very kind Egyptian host of a week, but he would not take any of it. So I gratefully gave his wife one of my mother's silver bracelets which fitted her wrist perfectly.

About 15 minutes later, Ahmad placed all my possessions on the train bound for Alex- andria.

Then, we two Ahmads (my Egyptian host and I) embraced each other, tears streaming down our faces.

A moment later, Ahmad got off the train as

it started moving slowly to take me to another city in my young life... to Alexandria, named after Alexander the Great of ancient Greece.

Someday in this life, or in the life to come after death, I hope with all my heart to meet two very kind men, my Iranian friend Reza and my Egyptian friend Ahmad... who saved my life from an untimely death.

Two days later I bought the last passenger ticket for the good Egyptian ship "Al Sudan" leaving Alexandria for New York. I paid my fare in very beautiful American Dollars.

The following morning, I left my Alexandria hotel room and moved into an old building across the street, which was operated by a friendly Lebanese as a weekly lodging home away from home. There I ate two meals a day, made my bed, washed dishes and scrubbed the floor, for about one third of what the hotel across the street was charging me.

The owner of the lodging place also directed me to a secondhand shop where I bought my first camera (loaded) for one very rich American Dollar.

He also introduced me to one of his tenants, a very nice 19 year old Italian-German newcomer to Alexandria who took me around Alexandria on foot and on tram, almost every day. It was a sincere friendship with a bit of romance, just a bit, at the beach.

Finally, my departure day arrived, February 7, 1947, a very clear and pleasant day.

At 10:00 a.m. I embraced my Lebanese landlord and my blue-eyed girlfriend of 18 days, who was weeping with sincerity that I have never felt from any other girlfriend since that day. Nevertheless, she was not meant to be my future eternal wife, but only a sweet dear friend.

About 20 minutes later, with a loaded suitcase in each hand, jacket pockets containing my passport, my money and important documents... and a French beret on my head... I climbed the stairs of the portable wooden ladder leading to the main deck of "Al Sudan", the Egyptian ship that was to take me about 6,000 miles to New York City.

When I stepped onto the ship, the uniformed Egyptian commander, a large, bronze-faced man about 50 years old, looked at my ticket and passport. Then he smiled and said to me,

"Ahmad, you are the last passenger. Welcome aboard."

Then the four uniformed police officers

standing around him, pulled the 40 foot ladder up onto the deck of the 14,000 ton ship. The captain motioned to me to join all the other passengers and ship crew who crowded almost every square foot of the large afore section of the deck.

Moments later the Commander of the ship, surrounded by the four police officers ... three men and a woman, stood on a wooden platform about a foot high.

The Commander proceeded to address us in a clear, deliberate manner (with a distinct Egyptian accent) as I stood about 20 feet from him. Looking at our faces quietly and earnestly, he said, "I am the captain of this ship, "Al Sudan", Egypt's second largest and most reliable ship after the flag ship, Al Maser(The Egypt)."

He looked at all of us even more intently and resumed saying, "You are now... and until you embark... on Egyptian territory and under Egyptian law. And I am your Captain and your friend. There are 638 passengers on this ship, myself, an excellent physician and a very good nurse, my two capable assistants... and these four tough ship police officers."

Only one person laughed at the remark of the "tough ship police officers"... the rest of us kept dead silent.

Then our captain continued, "We are now a big family... on a ship not so big. It makes no difference to me and my crew if you are a Muslim (Moslem), a Christian, or a Jew. There is no difference at all whether you are an Egyptian, a Lebanese, a Turk or a lone Iraqi (and with that he looked at me sympathetically); whatever you are... as long as you follow my rules you are equally honored and served."

Then he became stern and added, "But do remember to eat and sleep in your assigned area. If you are the holder of a third class ticket, you eat and sleep in the third class area. Do carry your passport and ticket with you at all times: even when you are sleeping."

Then he added, "There are 28 children under 12 on this ship. There are 138 women. There will be no abuse of any child or woman on this ship. There will be no fights, no stealing, no alcohol consumption, and no gambling allowed on this ship. If you are in third class, you stay where you belong. If you feel sick or are not feeling well, our good doctor (who never gets sea sick I hope... and at that many laughed momentarily), will be available day or night. Likewise, our good nurse will also be available. None of you is allowed to lean overboard more than two inches and each of you will put on your life jacket when I order you to do so."

Then he added, "Unfortunately, this good ship has a small jail room – doubly padded. I hope none of you will violate any Egyptian law or any of the orders I have given you. If you do, you may suffocate in the windowless jail room."

Then he ordered, "Now each of you must go to your assigned cabin or bunker. Do it quickly before some of you begin to feel sea-sick in the following 30 minutes."

The captain continued, "Now you are free to attend to your needs and get acquainted with your assigned sleeping area, eating area, your shower and restroom."

Immediately I grabbed my two suitcases and learned from one of the police officers that since I was the last passenger to get aboard with a third class ticket, that I was assigned to sleep in Bunk #100 on the basement level. He pointed me to the steps which would take me down... way down to my new and strange surroundings.

After descending to the first class level, then to the second class level, then to the base-ment level (assigned to third class passengers),

I quickly learned what it means to be a third class passenger on a passenger ship in 1947.

I quickly checked the wooden framed bunks and located my assigned bunk, #100. It was the upper one of two identical bunks, about five feet above the wooden floor.

I placed my suitcases on my army like bunk: a thin mattress about two feet wide and six feet long with two white sheets, a white pillow and a green blanket. Then I hurried to the restroom, which had four open showers with no door and no curtain, and six wash basins. I felt and tasted the water; hot and cold, yes... but salty.

When I returned to my bunk, I saw a young man placing his two suitcases on bunk #99, exactly below my bunk. He introduced himself politely, and I did likewise. I learned that his first name was Artugral, and that he was 20 years old, a student from Haran, a small town in Southeastern Turkey (only about 200 miles from Mosul). He also was on his way to America to enroll at Michigan State University. He looked about 160 pounds (22 pounds heavier than me). He looked a little pale to me.

Artugral also learned similar information about me and said in his limited English (much more limited than mine), that he had been suffering from a lingering flu he had caught when he came to Alexandria about ten days earlier, and that he was glad that I was his bunk mate.

A couple of minutes later, I climbed the 14 steps on each level up to the spacious deck and stood resting my arms on the five foot high deck rail...looking below to see if my blue-eyed girl friend was still there.

In a moment, I saw her gazing at the ship as if somehow to see me (her Romeo as she used to call me). I then took out my white handkerchief and began waving it at her and my Lebanese landlord. They recognized me too and began waving their hands unceasingly.

About two minutes later, the Al Sudan began moving out of its berth, slowly and majestically, blowing its two horns in a steady farewell... while I was blowing kisses to my girlfriend of 18 days in exchange for hers... until we disappeared from each other's sight.

By then, the Al Sudan had left the harbor and was steadily increasing her speed into the blue waters of the Mediterranean Sea.

Then, a short time later, the ship began turning from her Northerly course, to a Northwestern course. As she made the distinct change, I too began to feel a change in my head and in my stomach. I knew I was getting seasick.

Immediately, the middle-aged man (with his long black beard, black long robe, and black head piece) who was standing next to me, noticed my apparent condition and asked me, "Are you feeling well?"

I answered, "I think I am getting seasick."

Then he turned to his wife at his left and said something to her in Yiddish, and immediately she gave me a small bottle, about three inches tall and two inches wide. She opened the bottle and said to me, "Here, smell this. Take a deep breath. Trust me, it will help you."

She and her husband looked at me assuringly, and I followed her instructions, and inhaled twice. In less than 15 seconds, the dizziness suddenly decreased and I said to the man and his wife, "Thank you very much. I do feel better."

They smiled, gladly, and the wife said, "This is my own cure for seasickness. I hope it works for us too, if we need it."

By then I was feeling normal, and... curious as usual... I asked her, "What is it made of?"

She replied, almost whispering, "Fresh garlic juice and fresh onion juice."

Then the husband asked me, politely, "Where are you from?"

I answered, "I am from Mosul, Iraq."

Suddenly the woman screamed, "And I am from Mosul, Iraq too."

She came and hugged me as if I was her son.

After a moment, the woman screamed again, "I know you. You are the boy who used to pass by our house in Mosul, morning and afternoon. Did you go to King Ghazi Jr. High School in Mosul?"

I replied, beaming with happiness for this unexpected meeting, "I did."

Then the husband drew closer to me and confided quietly, "I was the Jewish Rabbi in Mosul. We lived next door to your junior high school for two years. But four years ago we moved to Baghdad."

I asked him, very interested to know more. "Did you just come from Baghdad?"

His wife replied, "When the persecution against the Jews in Baghdad became too much for us, we came to Cairo last year. But now we are going to live in New York."

So I asked her husband, somewhat boldly, "Rabbi, I noticed there are many men on the ship who have long beards and black head-pieces. Are there other Jews on the ship?"

He answered with a broad smile, "One hundred fifty-eight passengers, including Rasheel and I."

Now Rasheel, his gracious wife, opened a small zippered bag on her left arm, and pulled out a bottle identical to the one I inhaled from earlier, and with a smile said to her husband, "Yaakoob (Jacob), I am going to give this bottle to our new friend from Mosul."

I replied, "My name is Ahmad Rahawi."

The Rabbi, truly startled, announced, "I had a good Moslem friend in Mosul named Abdul-Aziz Rahawi."

With a choked-up voice, I said, "He is my father."

After two and a half days at sea, in pretty good weather, we arrived at Naples, the leading Italian seaport on the Mediterranean Sea.

It was the afternoon of February 9th, but the air was free of fog and the sun as warm as a day in April in Mosul, Iraq.

The ship discharged 25 passengers (none Jewish according to the Rabbi), and was boarded by 28 new passengers (All Jewish immigrants to America, according to the Rabbi), but only four of the men had the same length of beard as the Egyptian Jews.

The following morning, our ship left Naples, and that afternoon we passed between two large islands, Corsica and Sardinia. The following day we anchored at the Spanish sea port of Barcelona; and again, as in Naples, no passenger or crew member... not even the captain... was allowed to step on shore. However, two Spaniards on board got off, and eleven passengers (all Jewish as I was informed by the Rabbi), came aboard.

The following afternoon, after lots of boxes of fresh food stuffs, fresh water for drinking, washing hands and faces (but not for bathing) were loaded onto our ship. Then our ship headed on a Southwesterly course in somewhat choppy water and heavy rain at times... until we anchored about a quarter of a mile from the Spanish shore at the Strait of Gibraltar, which separates the African continent from Spain by a mere 14 miles.

At Gibraltar, we learned that there was a huge storm in the East Central Atlantic Ocean, and it was decided by our wise captain and his two assistants that we would wait out the storm, anchoring in the relatively safer waters of the Strait of Gibraltar.

There we stood, my Turkish bunk-mate and myself, gazing for hours at the famous Rock of Gibraltar through a pair of powerful binoculars (which Artugral's father, a high-ranking government official, had given him) which he shared with me... along with other gifts. Suddenly we spotted through the binoculars, several wild monkeys jumping at the top of the Rock of Gibraltar, then literally sitting only inches from the 1000 foot drop to certain death below.

In fact, a couple of the monkeys, in spite of the windy day, began to make love to each other, totally unconcerned with the fact that my Turkish friend and I were watching them, and that we were two Moslems who did not approve of such activities in public. Oh well, the animals will be animals.

Finally, the morning of our third day at Gibraltar, our captain called all the passengers together at the afore deck, and everyone (except a few children with runny noses and one expecting Moslem mother from Pakistan), appeared dressed warmly, a few with life jackets on, including myself. Better to be ready, than be eaten by a whale, was my motto.

Then our captain, again accompanied by his two assistants, the ship's four police officers, the ship physician and nurse... stood upon the foot high platform and spoke to us loudly (in Arabic),

"I want to thank God and I want to thank each of you for a very safe and pleasant journey, so far. But now what shall we do? Shall we keep waiting, anchored in our spot as now, waiting for the Atlantic to become placid as a swimming pool... or shall we trust in God and begin our six to seven day course to New York, today?"

There was silence for several seconds. Then suddenly, one man, a six foot tall Egyptian in his late thirties, shouted in Arabic, "Captain, I have never crossed the Atlantic Ocean before, but I don't trust it. Are we sufficiently prepared for this risk?"

The captain, slightly annoyed, replied, "I believe we are well prepared, as much as I know how."

The man shouted back, "Captain, the Titanic, the most prepared ship in history, sank in this terrible Atlantic Ocean, taking with her 1500 passengers. I do believe we should not risk it now."

Now the captain was really annoyed, and

shouted back, "I have decided that the storm has subsided enough, and it is time for us to cross the Atlantic... trusting in our ship, our skills, and in the Merciful God."

Then he added, calmly, "Of course, if you want, we will be glad to see you swim to the Spanish shore, and perhaps wave 'Bon Voyage' to us from the top of that great rock," and he pointed to the Rock of Gibraltar with his extended right-hand finger.

The worried man replied (half serious, half joking), "Since I cannot swim, and I cannot speak Spanish, and since I hate to be called a coward for the rest of my life... I have no choice but to wish us all Bon Voyage as one of you."

At that, the two huskiest police officers went to him and lifted him up on their shoulders, to the applause and happy laughter of all of us, even our good captain.

About ten minutes later, we all felt the Al Sudan slowly shifting from idle into first gear, and a few minutes later she turned her bow toward the greatest harbor in the history of the world, New York City, about 3,400 miles due Northwest. The Al Sudan was, by the way, the first ship ever, flying the Egyptian flag that ventured to cross the Atlantic.

A few hours later, I sat with my Turkish bunk mate in the ship's dining room, eating what was left over from the ship's huge kitchen, by the first and second class passengers, who had priority over us (the poor 113 third class passengers). There were 23 female third class passengers (including four teenagers and the expecting Pakistani woman and her worried husband). All 23 of them, as well as the 90 male third class passengers, occupied the double bunks in the basement level. The females were separated from us males by a locked door.

That meal that Artugral and I were leisurely enjoying, was to be the last meal that Artugral would ever eat sitting in the ship's attractively kept dining room located on the second class passengers' level. Throughout the rest of the journey to New York, I became responsible for bringing and feeding all of Artugral's meals to him because he became more seasick than any other passenger.

By 3:00 p.m. of our first day crossing the Atlantic, our 340 foot long ship was battered by a sudden new storm with 25 foot high waves. By dinner time, many passengers were not interested in eating dinner in the dining room.

Almost half the third class passengers did not sit for dinner at the four 30 foot long tables. As for myself, it was only for a few moments that afternoon that I felt I may get seasick again. But each time, I inhaled from the small bottle of mixed garlic and onion juices... the ill feeling left me in a few moments. I was very thankful to the Rabbi's wife who gave me that precious bottle, and above all... thanks be to God... who did not want me to get sick, so that I could tell many others... as I am telling you now... of God's gracious mercies upon me to the degree that I never got seasick more than a couple of minutes during my first hour at sea, as I stated earlier.

However, I discovered two other very good reasons why I should not get sick. First... while feeding Artugral his meal that evening, he offered me two beautiful American Dollars, although I never asked him for such. After that meal, he proceeded to give me two beautiful American Dollars each time I brought him a meal and each time I assisted him (including helping him to the restroom). Well, after that I accepted the dollars gladly.

Then later that evening, I did the same for two more men in third class... for one dollar each (which was what they offered and I accepted cheerfully).

Also that evening, due to the high seas, over half the passengers were seasick, so I thought of another idea. Why not offer two deep inhalings for those who wished, from the magic of my little garlic plus onion bottle... for a mere one U.S. Dollar? Would it not be good to help my fellow passengers enjoy the sight of 25 foot waves coming at our ship as a Lion? Yes, I thought it was worth a dollar indeed.

I also thought of Saturday. Wouldn't it be good for me to help my fellow Jewish passengers have a peaceful meal in their cabin (dressed as wished) instead of the dining room, for two dollars per couple? I felt good about that too.

My inhaling service was fun and profitable as well. Just two minutes of inhaling from the magic bottle... for only a dollar, provided that   the inhaler, not I, decided if the mixture worked for him or her. There was no pressure selling, just a friendly service.

However, to play it safe and legal, I went to see the ship's captain in his cabin, accompanied of course, by one of the two police officers on duty (the other two were seasick).

I related to the captain my experience

with the anti-seasickness bottle. At first he thought it was ridiculous. So I left, but came back with a beautiful Lebanese girl, about 21 years old, who was going to meet her wealthy parents in New York, for an extended U.S. vacation before they returned to Bogota, Columbia and their real estate business.

Amelia, the Lebanese girl, accompanied me to see the captain. She told him of her positive experiences with my magic bottle and finally said to him, smiling as sweetly as Drew Barrymore in one of her extra sweet roles, "Captain, do you think I would give anyone a dollar if I was not getting my money's worth?"

Then she added, "Besides, captain, Ahmad doesn't accept the dollar unless the person is willing to give the dollar, so what is wrong with that?"

The captain thought for a moment, smiled and said, "I don't see anything wrong with that. Besides, I too believe the smell of garlic and onion can be strong enough to affect almost anyone."

Then he turned to me and said, "Where did you get the garlic? I know we don't have it on our food supply list."

I answered him respectfully, "The wife of

the Jewish Rabbi gave it to me, as a favor, to help me."

The captain, smiling, nodded his head and said, "If the Rabbi approved of it, it must be Kosher."

Amelia asked the captain sincerely, "What is Kosher?"

He replied, obviously not sure, "I think it means it is approved by God."

Then he got up, shook hands with Amelia, then me and said, "By the way, Ahmad, since you don't get seasick, would you like to help run errands for me and the ship's doctor? The nurse and two police officers are seasick and can't work."

Amelia asked, pretending innocence, "Will Ahmad get paid for this?"

The captain answered her, "Yes he will. By the way, you are quite a business woman."

Amelia replied, "I wish my dad could hear that."

And we left the cabin to watch the huge waves looking huge enough to capsize the ship... but only to fail because the wave before had lifted the ship high enough to escape capsizing.

About a minute after Amelia and I left the captain's cabin, we saw the Pakistani husband shouting in English, "My wife is in labor. She is going to die. Please help me. Please help me."

Immediately Amelia eyed me and said, "Ahmad, the nurse is sick. Will you take him and his wife to the ship's doctor? I will accompany you."

We both rushed to the basement, and about ten minutes later, Amelia was holding the laboring woman's right hand and I holding her head in my right arm while the ship's doctor delivered her first daughter... who was crying her head off. Her father was waiting in front of the doctor's office, raising his hands to heaven in prayer to Allah, to keep his wife and child safe.

The great Mid-Atlantic storm, with immense waves as high as 30 feet, raged about us for three more days and nights, causing almost 60 % of all the passengers to get seasick... including I am sorry to confess, some of those who inhaled of my garlic/onion bottle.

Finally, to our great relief, the terrible storm took her fury further North, and our brave ship began to enjoy the playful punches of small seven to eight foot waves.

Meanwhile, Amelia and I became a familiar sight to the captain, the ship doctor, and to many others. She was an exceptionally well dressed girl, a wealthy 21 year old from Colombia, and I a 20 year old student hustler from Iraq. She was smaller than me, fairer, and a little smarter... at least on the surface of things.

Then, at 8:50 p.m. on the evening of February 21, 1947 , our brave ship, the Al Sudan, became the first ship flying the flag of Egypt, to greet the Statue of Liberty... America's symbol of hope and freedom to untold millions.

That memorable evening, about 9:00 p.m., three starry-eyed and happy passengers (Artugral on the right, Amelia on my left, and myself in the center) stood in the 35 degree weather, gazing and laughing and marvelling at the millions of lights adorning the New York skyline. Surrounding us were dozens of Egyptian and European Jews (including the Iraqi Rabbi and his wife), weeping in joy for arriving at their new home of hope and freedom, and looking forward to a new life without persecution.

However, none of us were allowed to leave the ship that evening. We had to wait until the next morning.

That night, my last as a passenger of our beloved ship, I could not sleep, perhaps like other passengers.

Then about 2:00 a.m. I sat on my bunk, put on my jacket which I held in my arms every night of my 14 nights at sea, then took all my money from my left inside pocket and started counting the dollars that I had earned... in the course of my service activities aboard the ship.

I was surprised to find that I had received 340 dollars... exactly one hundred dollars more than I had paid for my ship fare. Then suddenly I felt a special sense of gratitude to the Rabbi and his wife. So I put 100 dollars in a white handkerchief and left the men's third class area quietly. A minute later, I knocked gently on the wooden door of Cabin #12 on the second class passenger level, where the Rabbi and his wife stayed.

A moment later, the Rabbi in his pajamas, opened for me, obviously surprised, and said, "Ahmad, are you sleepwalking?"

I replied quietly, but smiling, "No Rabbi, I don't sleep walk, but I do have a gift for you and your wife."

Then I handed him the handkerchief containing the 100 American Dollars. After a moment of open-eyed surprise, he hugged me as a proud father and said, tears welling in his brown eyes, "I love you Ahmad. Shalom."

I answered choking with the weight of my emotions, "I love you Rabbi and your wife too. Shalom."

Later that morning, after an early 6:30 a.m. breakfast for first class passengers, followed by a 7:00 a.m. breakfast for second class passengers, and an 8:00 a.m. breakfast attended by every single person in the third class section (men, women and children)... including my bunk mate Artugral and the Pakistani mother holding her infant daughter.

Then about 8:20 a.m. I felt a strong urge to say something to my fellow passengers, so I got up (to the surprise of many), and said,

"My dear friends, I wish each of you much happiness and success in America. Please forgive me, if any of you was disappointed with me or my garlic and onion seasickness cure."

Then I said, "If any of you want his dollar back, I will give it to him or her now... but if anyone wishes to pay me $10.00 for the bottle, please pass on the ten dollars to me now."

I then sat down, amidst applause and laughter. Then Artugral got up slowly and said in his limited English, "My friends, I

79

think my bunk mate, Ahmad, deserves $20.00 for his bottle."

Then, amid applause and more laughter, he gave me twenty dollars, and I gave him the magic bottle that never cured him of his seasickness.

About forty minutes later, I was all set for my turn to descend the ladder from the Al Sudan to touch American soil with my feet... and my lips.

Then suddenly, Amelia came from her first class cabin. She was dressed like a Hollywood movie star, enough to arouse the passions of any normal 20 year old young man... let alone an increasingly romantic Ahmad Rahawi.

Then Amelia said to me, in her irresistible way of using eye contact, "Ahmad, my darling, didn't you tell me you were the last passenger to step on the deck of the Al Sudan in Alexandria?"

I answered matter of factly, "Yes, I did."

Then she said, reaching for my chest, "Why don't we become the last passengers to leave this ship?"

And she started breathing in my face, with eyes full of passion, but I replied, "No way. The captain, his assistants and the police officers are checking every nook and cranny in the ship to be sure that every passenger has left the ship by 10:00 a.m. We were told that at breakfast, weren't we?"

But Amelia replied, "Ahmad, let us spend the next 45 minutes in the boiler room. No one will interrupt us there."

And before I said a word, she exposed the top of her milky white bosom, and I went with her to the boiler room.

She opened the door quietly as we went in. Then she said, her eyes alternating pure sincerity with blinding passion, "Ahmad, I want you to meet my parents who are waiting for me at the pier right now. I know they will love you."

I was completely flabbergasted... and she brought her large brown eyes closer to my face and whispered in my ear, "Ahmad, I want you to marry me in our palace in Bogota, Colombia. Ahmad, you deserve to be a millionaire, not a struggling foreign student in America."

Suddenly, there was a loud kick at the door and the door was pushed open and... there stood the captain with his two assistants.

Amelia and I, startled, immediately got up on our feet. Then the captain said to me, slowly, "Ahmad, what are you doing here? You have only 20 minutes to leave the ship... unless you want me to take you back to Egypt!"

Amelia, unperturbed, answered smiling with her rich girl confidence, "Captain, Ahmad and I were discussing your wonderful talents as a captain. Besides, Ahmad was the last passenger to come aboard your ship. Doesn't he deserve to be the last passenger to leave your great ship?"

The captain laughed heartily, as most Egyptians do, and answered Amelia (while pushing me out of the boiler room), "Your parents are waiting for you in your cabin. They are worried sick because we could not locate you."

Then immediately Amelia and I left the boiler room. On our way Amelia whispered to me, "Wait for me by the ladder. I'll be back in five minutes."

On my way to pick up my suitcases, I regained my senses and murmured to myself, "I have to escape from Amelia. I do not want to be married now."

Almost in panic, I grabbed my two suitcases and ran to the ladder, respectfully showing my passport and student visa to the U.S. immigration officer who was standing at the bottom of the ladder... and found myself on

American soil. Yes, I, Ahmad Rahawi, was actually standing on American soil.

But instead of kissing America's precious soil as I had planned to do... I looked back and saw Amelia and her parents at the top of the ladder and heard Amelia shouting to me, "Ahmad, wait for me."

But I was once again the Ahmad Rahawi who had come to America to learn, to study, and to love America... and be the man I hoped to become in America... not the husband of a wealthy heiress in Bogota, Columbia.

I immediately saw a taxi pull into the street in front of me. I motioned to the taxi driver, now five feet from me. He opened the window nearest me and said, "Where to?"

I opened the taxi's door to the back seat, placed my suitcases there, and jumped in, slamming the door shut as if a demon were chasing me.

Then, I took a deep breath and said calmly to the taxi driver, "Please take me to the least expensive hotel you know... but I can't pay you more than $7.00."

The taxi driver, a tough looking man about 50 years of age, started driving and said to me, obviously not liking my $7.00 limitation, "What are ya, a cheap skate or something?"

I replied, laughing, "No, but I love cheap old hotels like $4.00 a night!"

Then he said to me casually, "Where are ya from?"

I replied, "Iraq."

He asked, as he began making a left hand turn onto a street that had more cars than Mosul and Baghdad put together, "Iraq? Where in the heck is that?"

I replied, unruffled by his roughness and poor knowledge of geography, "Iraq is a large country in the Middle East, as big as California, but it has 100 times more dates than California."

He became interested, and replied, "Lots of dates? Ha! I like redheads!"

I laughed again, realizing that he misunderstood what kind of dates Iraq was famous for, so I replied, "No, not that kind of date, that you chat with, take to the movies and sometimes kiss. I meant dates, the kind that grow on palm trees and I love to eat!"

He laughed and said, turning onto another street, "I like to eat dates too. How much per pound in Araak?"

I replied, "Oh, about two or three pennies per pound."

He said, "It costs ten times more in Nu

Yuk."

I understood that he meant New York.

A minute later, he pulled in front of an old building and announced to me, "Here you are, 'La Marquez Hotel'. You owe me seven bucks."

I replied laughing, but serious too, "How about two dollars discount for me teaching you about Iraq?"

He laughed again and said, "Okay, five bucks."

Then he added, "You know, you are a helluva salesman!"

I laughed too, got out of the taxi, retrieved my two suitcases and put them on the street curb, slowly waving good bye to him.

He waved back to me and said, sounding as sincere as any man could sound, "Good luck to you in America."

I replied, sincerely, "Thanks for everything."

He waved again, reached to his left eye as if saluting me, and drove off.

Then I picked up my two suitcases and entered the wide open door of my first home for a night in the greatest city in the world... in the greatest nation in the world... on the most unique continent in the world.

And the United States of America acquired a new resident... who had come all the way from Mosul, Iraq.

6

Early Years in the U.S.A.
My First Name Becomes Steve

I stayed the day and night of February 22, 1947 at the Le Marquez Hotel, located somewhere in Manhattan, I know not where. All I remember now is that it was surrounded by very, very high buildings... including one they called the Empire State Building.

Everything seemed different from Iraq. The people were all in a hurry and the streets full of thousands of cars. The weather was very cold for me, particularly since I didn't have leather gloves, a top coat, or a scarf to keep me warm on that wonderful but cold day, my first day in the land of my dreams.

The next day I exchanged an antique carpet (which my mother had received from the Persian wife of the Governor of the Province of Mosul)... for a heavy sweater, warm winter coat, pair of warm leather gloves, and a pair of sturdy shoes.

Then, at noon, I bought my bus ticket to Chicago, Illinois via Pittsburgh, Pennsylvania and Cleveland, Ohio.

Two days and two nights later, I registered at the Y.M.C.A. near the Loop in downtown Chicago. I then telephoned Bisrat Theodore at her home telephone which she had given me in her letter while I was still in Mosul.

Bismat met me the following day... and what a happy meeting it was. I learned that she was getting married to a very good man whom she loved, and who loved her.

Bismat also encouraged me to keep in touch with her and her future husband, which I intended to do gladly.

Before we said farewell, I had the joy of placing on Bismat's left wrist the most beautiful gold bracelet that my mother gave me to give to Bismat, in gratitude.

Then Bismat took a taxi that evening to stay overnight at the home of her future parents-in-law in Parkridge, a suburb of Chicago. I had a feeling that, somehow, we would meet again... even though this has not come to pass for the past 55 years.

I have confidence, however, that the God of Heaven who brings others to bless our lives... will yet give me the privilege to greet Bismat Theodore (Smith, her married name) again... in this life or the next.

I continued my bus trip from Chicago to Denver in extremely cold weather for Ahmad Rahawi, who had never known 20 degrees cold... let alone the -23 degrees that greeted me on my first night in Denver, Colorado at 1:00 a.m.

My first day in Denver, I was introduced to a photographer / Reporter of The Rocky Mountain News, Denver's second daily newspaper. He interviewed me, hoping that the story would be approved by the editor for publication. Ten days later, my beaming photo... and an article of somewhat inaccurate comments (such as that I was an Arab, while in reality I am not... I am an Israelite by blood from the Tribe of Dan... but an Iraqi Moslem by birth), did appear in "TRMN".

A few days after my story and photo appeared in the newspaper, I registered at the University of Denver as a pre-medical student.

I became quite popular on campus, especially with a very nice teacher by the name of Miss Salzman, who started calling me Steve and also told everyone she could to call me Steve, instead of Ahmad... because Steve (in her opinion) was perfect for my personality and looks.

Well, Miss Salzman was right, because I too began to like being called Steve. And by the end of six months at D.U. (The University of Denver), I was known as and called "Steve Rahawi" (which became my legal name when I became a naturalized U.S. citizen later on in 1956).

Meanwhile, I gave away 12 gold and silver bracelets and earrings that my mother had given me, as gifts or for needed cash... and some started calling me Steve Silverman or Steve Goldman. So a girl would introduce me to another as follows: "This is Ahmad Rahawi, aka Steve Silverman or Steve Goldman."

Then, about 16 months after enrolling at the University of Denver, two very important events happened to me, dramatically.

First, my father, Abdul Aziz Rahawi, died in Mosul, Iraq at the age of 50, due to complications caused by his excessive smoking. He left three wives, ten orphaned children in Mosul... and an orphaned son by the name of Ahmad who became Steve... far away across the seas in the United States of America. I never saw him again from the day he kissed me farewell. Thus my father died... uttering my Moslem name...Ahmad... as the last word of his earthly life.

The second event in importance happened shortly after my father's death. This was the fact that I had to combine my studies with a part-time job, subject to obtaining an employment permit from the immigration office in Denver, Colorado.

Subsequently, due to my changing circumstances, I changed my major to Business Administration, and about two weeks later, I obtained a permit to work from the Denver immigration and naturalization services... for which I was very grateful.

My first part-time job was washing dishes at the University of Denver's cafeteria. This resulted in my breaking several china dishes the first day, absolutely unplanned.

My second job (as a dog walker of a two year old bulldog) was no fun for me or the dog. So we parted company before the dog took a chunk of my leg in sweet remembrance of my firmness with his leash.

Fortunately, about three weeks after I received my work permit, I saw an ad for a full or part-time insurance salesman in the Denver Post. The position was to work for the C.H. Goodson Insurance Agency, located at 17th Street in downtown Denver.

Something whispered in my mind to "Go and see Charles H. Goodson. He will be like a father to you."

So, I quickly located the address, a few blocks from the immigration office, and 20 minutes later I was enjoying my first meeting with the first Mormon I had ever met. I learned that he was a high priest in The Church of Jesus Christ of Latter-Day Saints, and had eight children.

Fifteen minutes later, Mr. Charles Goodson, about 45, decided to employ me as a part-time insurance salesman... even though I had never heard the word "insurance salesman" in Iraq, had no car, and was carrying a full academic load at The University of Denver. But, he was determined to teach me, and I was very willing and eager to learn.

During the following 18 months, I had the privilege to receive good support from my new employer, Charles H. Goodson... to our mutual benefit.

Thus, I excelled at selling insurance, while managing to maintain a "B" or "B+" academic average, and often an "A" grade in certain scholastic courses. Why? Because where there is a will there is a way to success. I believe this is true for almost everyone in the world.

Another helpful factor in my insurance success was my commitment. "Never say Die." I simply kept going, doing my best, in spite of any apparent disadvantage... such as having to work without a car during my first year as an insurance salesman. I simply walked, and walked, and walked... miles and miles, or took the street car all over Metropolitan Denver.

One night at 11:00 p.m. in January, 1949, I couldn't even say "Hi" to the tram driver... my mouth was temporarily frozen because it was -24 degrees Fahrenheit in downtown Denver.

7

1st Marriage: Two Daughters, U.S. Citizenship, Then Divorce

By the middle of 1949, I had become a successful insurance agent, as a part-time salesman... while carrying a full academic load, as required by the U.S. Immigration rules for foreign students at U.S. universities and colleges.

I was working about 20 hours a week and earning $300 to $500 a week. By the middle of August 1949, I bought a brand new, fully equipped, deluxe, four-door Chevrolet Sedan and paid the full price of $2,320.00 in cold cash.

To make things more exciting for me, I was chosen as "1949 Top Sales Rep" of the 26 member sales force of the C.H. Goodson Insurance Agency. I did so well in a rather short time because I followed the instructions and suggestions of my very wise and encouraging boss, Mr. Goodson.

However, because I was spending about 90 hours a week between attending classes, studying and working part-time, as well as tending to the yard of my landlady (Mrs. Garfield) in exchange for my room... I hardly had any time for dating (even though I had the desire, the money, and a new luxury car). Moreover, I was not an expert on girls as most young men my age (23 years plus a month)... when I celebrated my first Christmas Day ever, inside a church.

Then came 12:01 a.m. of January 1, 1950, and three of my buddies at D.U. and myself (all without a date)... rose up on our feet as everyone else at the packed Rainbow Dance Room, a huge dance hall at Broadway and Cherry Hills Parkway in Denver, Colorado.

Minutes later, each of us four young bachelors made a solemn New Year's resolution (assisted by the influence of a bottle of beer), that each of us would be married by the next New Year's Day. And I fully intended to fulfill that resolution, no matter what.

Two weeks following the day of our New Year's resolution, all four of us were studying at about 3:00 p.m. at the nice and quiet library of D.U.'s upper campus. Suddenly, I saw a fair young woman with beautiful hair, blue eyes, and the smallest waistline that I had ever noticed... even with my ever-opened eyes for good looking women.

In a moment, this beautiful light brown-haired beauty came and sat at an unoccupied study table, next to our table... we marriage-oriented, hot blooded, good looking D.U. students, aged 23, 23, 20 and 22.

After several unsuccessful tries to attract her attention, I got up and slowly but deliberately came and sat right in front of her... with only my Marketing Principles textbook separating the two of us.

Suddenly she said to me, "Where are you from?"

I answered, "I am a foreign student from Iraq majoring in Marketing with a B+ average. I am also the top salesman in a large insurance agency. I also own the fanciest car you have ever seen. You can call me Steve... or Steve Rahawi... or Steve Reno... as you like best. How about you?"

She peered at me, with the shadow of a smile, and replied with a Southern accent, "My name is Marguerite. I am a graduate student in Psychology, on the G.I. Bill because I was in the army for two years."

Then she stopped and almost went back to her studies, but I looked at her carefully and was so enticed by her blue eyes and her tasteful appearance, that I ventured forth and said, "Marguerite, you have a beautiful name. Would you like to see how I drive my fancy car? How about a date tomorrow for a movie, or dancing, or dinner?"

She looked at me as if she was going to buy me, then said, "How about a double date with my roommate Lucy and her fiance Cas? I live a few blocks from here."

I replied, laughing, "This is meant to be. I live on South Washington Street only ten blocks from here. How about 7:00 p.m. tomorrow... my first Friday off in 20 months?"

She smiled again and said, "What is your Iraqi first name?"

I replied, "Ahmad."

She answered, "I will see you, Ahmad, and your fancy car tomorrow at 7:00 p.m.."

Then she got up and left.

Friday evening, I met Marguerite and Lucy and Cas, as agreed, and 20 minutes later all three of them were screaming every time I drove my Chevy between the two cars in front of me... literally missing each car by a few inches. Yes, I drove that way... but never had a collision.

The four of us, myself, Marguerite, and

Cass and Lucy had several dates together, and we became well acquainted. The three of them learned how confident and romantic (and ignorant) a student from Mosul, Iraq, could be.

Marguerite and I became "steady" and I picked her up regularly from her part-time employment at Brookenridge Farms, about five miles away, because she did not have a car.

Marguerite was three years older than me, wiser, slower, far more intellectual, more argumentative, and a typical liberal American girl... She grew up in Savannah, Georgia as an orphan since her mother died when Marguerite was eight. She was also very neat, never a deliberate liar, nor an extravagant person.

I liked her and felt proud to be with her, but I never heard her say to me, "I love you," and I did not feel she actually did love me with the true, deep and unchangeable love I thought I deserved.

Nevertheless, all in all, she was the best prospect for me to marry in 1950.

So we were married in July of 1950 in a civil ceremony, not in a mosque nor in a church, and not by any kind of clergyman. But then, neither one of us apparently cared.

Thus Marguerite and I began our married life... I as a senior in Marketing at The University of Denver's downtown campus, and she as a graduate student at the University Park campus.

We both continued working part-time, spending most of our time attending classes and studying two different fields; neither of us caring for the other's field of interest.

We continued to be incompatible intellectually, and I discovered a few months later that spiritually we were not compatible at all.

I graduated by the end of the school year in June 1951, and continued to break sales records (and continued to work until about 10:00 p.m. selling insurance), which further reduced our social life and compatibility.

Then on November 16, 1951, I took Marguerite to Rose Memorial Hospital in East Denver to deliver our first child.

After hard labor of 35 hours, the attending nurse came to me in the waiting room (I never knew it was good for a husband to be with his wife at delivery time), and told me full of smiles, "You've got the cutest baby I have ever seen, and your wife is doing well."

Three days later, holding our daughter in my right arm and my wife (still a little weak) with my left hand, the three of us went as a family to our apartment at 380 South Cook in South Denver.

Then I finished 1951 with another gift from God. I was named the Top Insurance Agent, nationwide, for World Insurance Company of Omaha, Nebraska (a health and life insurance company with over 600 sales representatives).

Two months later, I was asked by my Boss, C.H. Goodson, to become his junior partner in the State of Utah. I refused the offer and instead, accepted to become General Agent for World Insurance Company in Oklahoma.

So Marguerite (and Susan, our beautiful little daughter) and I moved to Oklahoma City and purchased an attractive new home, complete with its own running creek.

Two months later, I was chosen by the national magazine "Direct Selling" as The 1951 National Direct Salesman of the Year, with a two-page centerfold article.

Later on, Marguerite and I were blessed with another beautiful blue-eyed girl on December 5, 1954. She was born about 10 days earlier than expected, at Mercy Hospital in Oklahoma City. Sadly, I was working that day when Marguerite was rushed to the hospital, by one of my salesmen and his wife.

Again, three days later, we left Mercy Hospital in Oklahoma City, with me carrying our beautiful new daughter, Patricia, in my right arm, and holding her still weak mother in my left hand... we went home and introduced tiny Patricia to her big sister, Susan, who was three years and 17 days older.

In the following three and a half years, I developed a small, but profitable and quality insurance agency for World Insurance Company, and trained many salesmen, one of whom was Jim from Tulsa, Oklahoma. He quickly learned how to become a Top Dog, and did become the top agent for the company nationwide in 1957.

I also continued to spend most of my time concentrating on my business, seven days a week, (with little time for my family)... seeking to make more and more money and traveling all over Western Oklahoma.

In 1956 I had the great privilege and joy to become a naturalized U.S. citizen. I raised my right hand before witnesses (and God) and swore that I would honor my pledge to the flag of the United States of America... a flag I love to salute and honor with all my heart.

Although everything seemed to be going good for us, Marguerite was unhappy in many ways. So in July of 1958, I sold my business to World Insurance Company, sold our house, and drove to Denver, Colorado in my two year old Chevy (with Patricia in the back seat), while Marguerite in our newer station wagon (with Susan next to her) followed 100 feet behind me... to start a new, and hopefully happier life.

By this time, my wife had become active in a group that denied the divinity of God, Jesus Christ, and the prophets; and worse than that, I had become an arrogant businessman who never gave thanks to the Lord God who had brought me to America, and who had been so generous to me. I became a man guilty of many sins, a man who gave his wife and children luxury but not companionship.

Our home was a beautiful place on the outside, but irritable on the inside. There was never a blessing at mealtime, never a mention of God or Jesus Christ to our children, never a family prayer, or any prayer. There was never a thought or discussion or hope of eternal family ties. Instead, I had a growing nagging fear in my mind and in my heart, that eventually my wife would divorce me, and I would be denied normal fatherhood to my two precious daughters.

Two months later, after I had sold my insurance business in Oklahoma City, I became a state manager in Denver, Colorado for another national insurance company... and started to compete with my former mentor, Charles H. Goodson.

About a year later, Charles H. Goodson and I met in a parking lot, unexpectedly. He looked me in the eyes and quietly said, as a loving father to his wayward son, "Steve, reconsider your ways. Reconsider your life, before all you have built collapses. Why don't you consider what I told you before. Your future is in Salt Lake City, as my junior partner."

With utter ingratitude, I replied, "Charles, I don't need your advice. I am going to compete with you and your son, Grant. I am going to become wealthy."

He gave me a long look and said, "The choice is yours." And he drove away.

A few days later, my house doorbell rang. I opened the front door to see a Deputy Sheriff, who said to me, "Are you Mr. Steve A. Rahawi?"

When I answered, "Yes", he said to me, "Mr. Rahawi, you have 20 minutes to leave this house. Your wife has filed for divorce, and this is a court order."

At the same time, I heard my wife run to her new Oldsmobile station wagon and rocket out of our double car garage.

That night, one of the most miserable in my life on this earth, I stayed in a motel room. At midnight, I wept with the realization that I would no longer... be able to check, every night, that my daughters were sound asleep... before I myself went to sleep.

8

Free to Believe

About three years later, at the age of 37, I was a divorced man... living in a hotel room near downtown Denver, but traveling often to California seeking, without success, funding for a new health insurance company I wanted to incorporate in Colorado or California.

After returning to Denver one evening, exhausted from a useless trip to San Francisco, in my old Oldsmobile with its 150,000 miles, (I used to have a new car almost every year), I exited my car, alone, on 17th Street in downtown Denver, saying to myself, "Look at me at age 37... no wife to greet me with love, no children to hug and play with at will, one wrong girlfriend after another, my $40,000 business bank account has dwindled to less than a thousand with no prospects for income, my days full of tension and my nights sleepless; I drink five to eight cups of coffee a day, yet my stomach is constantly nervous. What a life!" And I started weeping in despair.

On my way to my hotel room, I bought a copy of The Denver Post, and when I arrived at my room, I sat on the edge of my bed and opened the newspaper at random.

My eyes instantly focused on a full page article entitled "The Mormons Claim that Joseph Smith Did See God and Jesus Christ... Standing next to Each Other."

And at the left-hand margin of the article, there was a small photograph of a distinguished old gentleman smiling and a smiling elderly lady sitting with him. Under the photograph was written, "David O. McKay, Mormon Prophet, celebrates his 92nd birthday with his wife, Emma."

Never before had I ever read anything that impressed its importance upon my mind as this newspaper article. When I finished reading it, I made up my mind to do all I could... to find out if Joseph Smith truly did see God and Jesus Christ, standing next to each other. And if the Book of Mormon that was described in the article was truly the Word of God or the made-up writings of Joseph Smith, I also wanted to know if the man David O. McKay was a true prophet of God or not.

The next evening, I went alone to see a movie entitled "Around The World in 80 Days,"

and as I saw on the screen what was called...
The Great Salt Lake Valley... I heard (either
physically, or by inspiration) the most wonderful choir I ever heard, singing a wonderful
hymn... saying "Come, Come, Ye Saints, no toil
nor labor fear, but with joy wend your way."

The hymn pricked my heart so deeply that
when I left the theatre, I couldn't remember
where I had parked my car. That night I resolved to drive to Salt Lake City, Utah, the
world headquarters of the Church of Jesus
Christ of Latter-Day Saints.

I arrived in Grand Junction, Colorado
the next evening, which was only a short
drive from Utah. And that night, about 2:00
a.m., I knelt on my knees in my motel room,
and prayed to the True Eternal God... for the
first time in my life... asking him to help me
know why I had such a great desire to know
the truth about Joseph Smith and the Book
of Mormon, and David O. McKay.

About ten hours later, I got out of my car
only a few feet from a metal sign that read,
"Welcome to Utah." And I raised both hands
high towards heaven and pleaded to God to
lead me on.

As I live now and write these words, I testify that the moment I drove my car, into the

State of Utah, I felt like... I had come home.

That night I stayed in Price, Utah and the next morning I came to Thistle Junction, and something in me encouraged me to drive South on Highway 89... to the small towns of Southern Utah, and I did so.

Never in all my travels was I greeted by so many friendly people, everywhere I stopped for gas or food or a drink of water. One older man, sitting next to me in a little restaurant, asked me after chatting a few minutes, if I was a single man. When I replied "Yes", he said, with a cheerful smile, "Come to our home for dinner tonight. I have four beautiful single daughters."

Unfortunately, I was not in tune enough, so I thanked him and kept driving South, to see a while later the most spiritually inspiring building.

When I stopped by an entrance to this magnificent building, I saw it was named "The Manti Temple". And as I stood under a tree on the temple grounds, I bowed my head before God and begged Him to lead me on.

That evening, about 8:30 p.m. I stopped at a small motel called "The Sands" in the Northeast part of a small town called Panguitch.

After I paid room rent for one night, the

middle-aged motel clerk asked me, with a friendly smile, "What are you doing here in Panguitch, Utah?"

I answered, smiling too, "Well, I want to know the truth about Joseph Smith... and the Church of Jesus Christ of Latter-Day Saints, and its Book of Mormon."

The motel clerk's eyes twinkled and she said to me quietly, "I know the church is true. I have been a member of it all my life."

Then she added, with an even greater gleam in her eyes, "There is a copy of the Book of Mormon in your room. You might as well get acquainted with it tonight." Then she gave me my room key, with another friendly smile, as gentle as the dew from heaven.

After I had dinner, I returned to my room and sure enough, there on the lamp table by the bed, I saw The Book of Mormon for the first time in my life.

I picked up the book, reverently, in both hands, then I opened it at random. Immediately my eyes locked onto a verse that seemed to stand out as a blazing light. It was Verse 6 in Chapter 33 of 2Nephi, which read, "I glory in plainness, I glory in truth, I glory in my Jesus, for He hath redeemed my soul from hell." Suddenly, I felt very sweet peace.

Then, between 10:30 p.m. of that evening of May 14, 19 65 and 2:00 a.m. of the morning of May 15, 1965, I slowly read every word from the title page of the book to the end of Chapter 13 of 1 Nephi.

Then, I, Steve A. Rahawi, a very unreligious man at the time, about 2:30 a.m. of that May 15, 19 65, did go down on my knees in sincere prayer, with real intent (having faith in Jesus Christ, as the Son of God)... and I asked God, the Eternal Father (Elohim)... if Joseph Smith told the truth about seeing God and his Son, Jesus Christ standing together? Whether the Book of Mormon was truly another Testament of Jesus Christ? And if Joseph Smith did translate the Book of Mormon, by the power of God, from ancient Egyptian to English? And if David O. McKay was a Prophet of God?

And I testify that early morning I knew I had found the faith, the Church, and the way of life I wanted to live as a follower of my Lord and Savior, Jesus Christ.

Less than six months later, on the evening of November 3, 1965, I was baptized by complete immersion for remission of my sins, in the baptismal font on the Westside of the

Tabernacle on Temple Square in Salt Lake City, Utah.

About an hour later, I was confirmed a member of The Church of Jesus Christ of Latter-Day Saints, and immediately the gift of the Holy Ghost was bestowed upon me, and I received it with great joy and gratitude.

Another hour or so later that very memorable evening of my earthly life, about 30 Latter-Day Saints of the Monument Park 14th Ward in Salt Lake City, celebrated with me a wonderfully joyful Kentucky Fried Chicken dinner in the Sugar House area on 21st South Street in Salt Lake City, one of the most beautiful cities in the United States of America... where everyone is free to choose. I chose to follow Jesus Christ... as my Savior, my Redeemer and my Advocate with God the Eternal Father.

Four days later on November 7, 1965, looking and feeling like a new man born of God, I found myself standing at the entrance to the L.D.S. Chapel (some people say Mormon, because of the church's use of the Book of Mormon as another Testament of Jesus Christ), located at Pearl and 7th Streets in Denver. Suddenly I felt a hand upon my shoulder, and when I looked, I saw the eyes of the first Latter-Day Saint I ever met... the eyes of my first employer, the eyes of Charles H. Goodson, looking at me. His eyes were wide open as he said to me smiling, "Steve Rahawi! What are you doing here?"

I smiled back to Charles, and shook his big right hand, answering happy as a lark, "Brother Goodson, I am now a member of the Church."

9

2nd Marriage: A Daughter, A Son, then Divorce

On June 24, 1967, at the age of 38 years, I drove from Denver, Colorado to Salt Lake City, Utah to find a wife... within 100 days. A pretty large trailer containing my personal and business belongings, was hitched to my four year old Oldsmobile.

Ten days later, I was introduced by Gwen (the wife of Joe, my first friend in the city), to her hairdresser.

The hairdresser was a very well groomed and attractive 29 year old, who had arrived in Salt Lake City as an immigrant from Finland. However, she couldn't speak much English... a good opportunity I thought to teach her the type of English I liked best.

She also had two beautiful blonde children, a seven year old son and a six year old daughter. This attractive hairdresser was a divorced woman from a man who lived in Finland.

Well, I thought to myself, "I have always

liked Finland and its people, based on what I have studied. Besides, if I marry Tuovi, I would certainly have a clean and orderly home, never mind the fact that her two children were somewhat uncooperative."

After daily dating and much debate in my mind, I proposed to Tuovi, and she accepted gladly. We were married on October 5, 1967, exactly 100 days from my arrival in Salt Lake City.

After a two day honeymoon, all four of us (and all our belongings packed into a large trailer hitched to my car), drove to Denver where I was to start a new job, as the Colorado State Manager for Surety Life Insurance Company of Salt Lake City, Utah.

During the next two years, I regained my sales powers and led the 500 insurance/mutual fund sales reps of Surety Life.

Six months later, our first child, Sonja Elisabeth, was born during a relatively easy childbirth in a peaceful hospital in Englewood, a suburb of Denver. Sonja was both beautiful and healthy and a joy to hold in our arms... and her siblings loved her.

A year later, we returned to Salt Lake City and bought a house that sat on top of a cliff, in a typical, friendly and clean neighborhood of Salt Lake City called Canyon Rim Stake.

I continued selling insurance and mutual funds in Salt Lake City, while serving as a Host at the world famous Temple Square... and what a wonderful experience it was! I believe I hosted over 50,000 visitors from many countries, including some special VIPs, Senator Strom Thurmond of South Carolina, the Minister of Education of Morocco, and a very friendly rabbi from Israel.

After two and a half years in Salt Lake City, during which I did not do so well in my business, I accepted the company offer for me to become a General Agent in Sacramento, California. So all five of us went to California with anticipation.

During our first two years in Sacramento, living in a nice rented three bedroom, two bath apartment, I again led the entire company sales force, both in volume of life insurance sold and in premiums collected. For this I was awarded a new car as a bonus.

Meanwhile in Sacramento, I, my wife, two stepchildren, and smart little Sonja were active in our church. All was going very well.

Then a terrible tragedy struck all of us. About 1:00 a.m. on a blistery night in March of 1974, I rushed my wife to a hospital in Sacramento to deliver our expected son.

The obstetrician was somehow unavailable, so he sent his younger, less experienced partner. An hour or so later in the delivery room, while my wife's head rested on my right arm... my wife's uterus ruptured, and all the instruments attached to her body went completely dead. They rushed her to the emergency operating room where her regular obstetrician finally arrived.

About two hours later, both physicians came to me in the waiting room, and sheepishly advised me that my wife was critical and my son had suffered a spinal injury.

Immediately I phoned the two full time missionaries, Elder Smith and Elder Steele, to come quickly that the three of us may exercise the authority of the Holy Priesthood in us vested.

Both arrived in less than 40 minutes and the three of us, united in prayer of faith, did ask and receive the physician's permission to annoint and bless my wife. The child had been transferred to another hospital.

After we did annoint and bless my wife... by the power of the Holy Melchizedek priesthood in us vested... with complete faith in the

Father and in the Son and in the Holy Ghost, my wife began to breath on her own. Seconds later her eyes opened.

Three days later, Tuovi ate a full hospital meal and she was smiling and combing her hair. Two weeks later, she went with me and the older children to all three Sunday meetings in our chapel... looking as healthy and well groomed as ever.

However, our beloved son, Dan Joseph, after 80 days in intensive care in Sacramento and Salt Lake City hospitals, and eight days in our personal care, died very peacefully and silently in a chiropractic clinic in Wisconsin... our last futile effort to prolong his life.

My wife and I, with some of our close friends in Salt Lake City, buried Dan Joseph in a most beautiful spot beneath the peaks of the Wasatch Mountains and overlooking the Great Salt Lake Valley.

During the 89 days Dan Joseph was alive, I spent almost all my time, attention, love and prayers for him... to such a degree that it generated great jealousy and resentment on the part of my 14 year old stepson. With his intense jealousy of little Dan Joseph, he also manifested a great hatred toward me, accompanied by almost unbelievable defiance and hostility. Unfortunately, I responded in kind... instead of using wisdom, patience and love.

After almost two years of such behavior, which made life miserable for all of us, one afternoon my wife announced to me, "You two will never live together. I have had enough of this. I want a divorce."

I knew she had made up her mind.

A few days later, our beloved and loving five year old daughter, Sonja, suffered a broken leg and was confined to a Sacramento hospital for many days.

With all these calamities piling on top of each other, compounded by very large hospital bills, far exceeding my insurance coverage... I became overwhelmed and could not muster the strength, desire and self assurance needed for my insurance sales. I became in debt for the first time in my life.

About two years after Dan Joseph's death, I had wiped out all my savings and the money I received from Surety Life in exchange for my future renewal income from my insurance sales. I was crippled financially, surrounded by an alienated wife, two hostile stepchildren, and unable to work.

Then one black day in May of 1976, I

came home about 6:00 p.m. from a futile business trip to find our family's large apartment completely empty of everything... except a mattress on the floor, my personal clothing, books and a few kitchen items. There was no note, no explanation, no way for me to know where my wife of eight and a half years and the three children had gone.

But as I knelt in prayer, asking guidance and comfort, I knew that my second marriage was about to end forever. And again I wept for the loss of my son, Dan Joseph, and my beautiful five and a half year old daughter, Sonja, the peacemaker who had tried but could not make peace endure in our shattered family.

Three days later, I discovered that my estranged wife and three children had moved only about a mile away. Nevertheless, several attempts for reconciliation failed. Accordingly, on the advice of my Bishop (a man of God whom I honored), I left Sacramento, California on December 3, 1976 to move to Salt Lake City, Utah. I was driving a small rented trailer that contained all my personal and business belongings (because I had to surrender my almost new car for my inability to make monthly payments due to my heavy debts).

About two hours later, as the evening sun

was kissing the snow covering the hills atop Donner Pass, near the California-Nevada State line, I felt loneliness like never before, as I drove on to Salt Lake City, Utah.

10

Forming and Managing "The American-Arab Foundation"

During the following two years, I worked as a General Agent in Salt Lake City, for a Texas insurance company, sending the agreed upon monthly child support, for my daughter Sonja and step-children. I continued to do so for many years, until each of the three children reached their 21st birthday.

Meanwhile, my second divorce became final under California law, and my second wife married another man six days later. Perhaps he was not as good looking as I was, but he had a much easier last name to pronounce than mine. So she became Mrs. Baker instead of Mrs. Rahawi. Then, about a year after she became Mrs. Baker, she obtained about $120,000 through a medical malpractice court judgment for her suffering and the subsequent death of our son, Dan Joseph. I did not get a penny from that money.

Shortly after, being an advocate of good-will and friendship between my country of choice and citizenship... the U.S.A.... and the land of my birth, Iraq (as well as other Arab oil producing nations), I formed, with a lot of hard work and good support, a national, public supported foundation called "The American-Arab Foundation".

The foundation was headquartered in Salt Lake City for its first two years, with a Board of Directors of ten.

Then in June of 1980, at a meeting of the Foundation's Board of Directors, it was decided that I should go to Washington, D.C. to seek contributions from the embassies of Arab oil producing nations.

Two days later, I boarded a night flight to Washington, D.C. via Denver, Colorado. About seven hours later, I was on my way to a hotel in Washington, D.C. It was my first time to visit the greatest and most important capital in the world.

The next afternoon, I entered the wide open door of the Embassy of Saudi Arabia, and introduced myself as Steve A. Rahawi, President of the American-Arab Foundation... a federally approved public supported foundation. I then proceeded to request the privilege of meeting His Excellency, the Ambassador of Saudi Arabia to the United States.

Twenty minutes later, I found myself standing in a very spacious office, shaking hands with Ambassador Alhegelan, a kind and gracious looking man.

In the following ten minutes, I explained in simple and sincere words, the program of the foundation, what it had already accomplished and hoped to accomplish. I then showed His Excellency some pictures of the first Anniversary banquet of the Foundation in Salt Lake City.

Thirty minutes later, I left the Saudi Embassy smiling and shaking hands with everyone... with a nice check of thousands of American Dollars in my left inside pocket. (I always use the left inside pocket for important papers, perhaps because it is good for my heart.)

Another hour later, I was at the Embassy of Qatar, and again I was welcomed and left with another several thousand dollars in contributions. I can honestly state that all the Qatar Embassy personnel were most hospitable.

About 11:00 a.m. the next morning, flush with confidence, I approached the guarded door of the main entrance of the Embassy of Iraq. And since I looked friendly and respectful, I suppose, I was ushered in as President of the American-Arab Foundation to meet with His Excellency, The Deputy Ambassador of Iraq.

In a minute, I was looking at a young man (about 35), a sharp looking Iraqi diplomat. He was holding a cigarette in his hand. Later I learned that the cigarette was an American brand (a Camel), not the leading Iraqi brand that my father used to distribute in Mosul.

Upon seeing me come in his office, he stood up, smiling with a little hint of over-confidence. Then he motioned to me to sit in a large, well upholstered chair, across from his large desk.

For about 30 seconds, we sat eyeing each other without a word. Then he said to me slowly, "Your surname, Rahawi, sounds Arabic. Where are you from originally?"

I replied politely, "Your Excellency, I was born in Mosul, Iraq. I came to the United States as a student in 1947 and became a naturalized American in 1956."

Then he asked me, smiling, "Do you like being a U.S. citizen?"

I replied, slowly and surely, "Indeed I do. I love America. To me America is the greatest democracy on earth."

Then he pressed a button on his desk, and

immediately a stout security guard appeared in the room, and the Deputy Ambassador said to him, "This is Mr. Rahawi. Bring him a cup of coffee."

And I answered, politely but resolutely, "Thank you, Your Excellency, but I don't drink coffee."

He then told the security guard, "Bring Mr. Rahawi a cup of tea!"

I said again, politely, "Thank you, Your Excellency, but I don't drink tea either."

He looked surprised, then told the security guard, "Bring Mr. Rahawi a coke."

I said again, "Thank you, Your Excellency, but I don't drink coke either."

Suddenly, he opened his hands wide, and replied as if pleading for an end to my objections, "Please tell me what do you like to drink?"

I answered, smiling politely, "Water will be just fine."

Then with apparent relief, he told the security guard, "A big glass of water for Mr. Rahawi."

In a minute, the security guard returned, walking slowly and carefully carrying a huge glass of water, which he placed very carefully before me because it was absolutely full to the top.

Then, to show the Deputy Ambassador that I really did like water, I took the longest sip in my life from that huge glass, until I thought I was about to drown. And the diplomat said with admiration, "You really like water, don't you."

I replied, almost out of breath, "Water is the best drink in the world."

He laughed heartily and said, "Mr. Rahawi, I like you. May I call you Steve?"

I replied, relieved to hear him say that, "Please do, and what shall I call you?"

He replied cheerfully and with obvious sincerity, "Call me Raaed."

Then he asked me seriously, "What can I do for you today?"

I replied, looking him straight in the eye, "Raaed, I would like the largest donation you can give me, today!"

He replied, sounding like an old friend, "Well you know that any substantial financial contribution to your foundation must be approved by Baghdad, but how about $2,000 today?"

I replied as graciously as I could, "I will gladly accept $2000 today."

Then he quickly dialed on the desk phone and I heard him say, "Ibrahim, make a check for $2000, payable to the American-Arab Foundation as a donation. I am taking the Foundation's President to lunch. We will be back in about an hour. Have the check ready."

About ten minutes later, Raaed and I (and the security guard) were seated for lunch at a nearby restaurant.

As we waited for our orders to be served, I said to the Deputy Ambassador, earnestly, "Raaed, I have a great desire in my heart."

He replied jokingly, "For Iraq to donate 10% of its oil revenue to your foundation?"

I replied jokingly, but hopefully, "Even one million a year would be great... but what I want to say now is not about a donation. It's about my belief that the United States and Iraq can become good business partners and friends."

He drew his face closer to me and whispered, "How is that?"

I replied, quietly but more earnestly, "America needs Iraq's quality oil, and Iraq needs America's know-how."

He looked at me thoughtfully, then said, "I would like that very much. The U.S. and

Iraq did over $1 billion dollars in trade last year. I hope it will become $10 billion in the future."

By then, the waitress came with our lunch and asked me, "Would you like a cup of coffee with your lunch?"

And immediately His Excellency, the Deputy Ambassador of Iraq, answered the waitress on my behalf, "No thanks... just a big glass of water for my guest."

The waitress looked surprised, but returned with a big glass of water (thankfully, only half as big as the one I was given at Raaed's office about 30 minutes earlier).

About 40 minutes later, back in his office, Raaed gave me the check for the $2,000 donation, and said quietly,

"I am returning to Baghdad in about a month. Why don't you come to see me there? I hope I can give you a much larger donation."

Then he added, "I like your efforts to create greater goodwill between America and Iraq." He then clasped my right hand.

A few minutes later, I left the Iraqi Embassy compound shaking hands and smiling to everyone... glad to be "An American Born in Iraq."

Unfortunately, two weeks after Raeed returned to Baghdad, the Iraq-Iran War broke out, and I never received another contribution from the Embassy of Iraq, and I never saw Raaed again because (I was told) he did not come back to Washington.

Several months later, I convinced the Foundation's Board of Directors to move the foundation's address to Washington, D.C., and the Board approved this move by a majority vote, as required by the foundation's bylaws.

Within a week I sold all my furnishings and my car. Then on January 23, 1981, accompanied by two suitcases (about 40 pounds each) and a briefcase containing valuable papers of the foundation and mine, I took a jet from Salt Lake City to Los Angeles International Airport, where I spent several hours visiting my daughter, Susan, her husband, and their one year old son and 15 days old daughter, in their beautiful Malibu home.

Then about midnight, I boarded another jet to my new home, Washington, D.C. Upon arriving in Washington, I checked into a hotel where I had stayed the past summer, using my spacious room both as an office and a bedroom.

About three weeks later, I became acquainted through mutual friends with an outstanding executive, at a social dinner. He was recently retired from the CIA as a top executive. Shortly after he accepted to be Executive Vice President of the Foundation.

Together we worked on a project to have an international dinner and program, at the Washington Hilton Hotel, to be attended by many Middle Eastern Ambassadors and selected government officials, as well as interested members of the U.S. Senate and U.S. House of Representatives. Our planning progressed well.

However, sadly for our nation and our planned event, President Ronald Reagan was seriously wounded in an assassination attempt, at the entrance of the same hotel we had chosen for our big event.

Subsequently, all our plans for the event were cancelled. However, during those several weeks, I did receive a $3,000 contribution from the Embassy of Qatar, which kept the foundation operating.

The next day I visited the Embassy of Algeria (next door to my hotel), and the Deputy Ambassador met me kindly. In a matter of minutes, I was told that His Excellency, The

Ambassador of Algeria would love to have me as his lunch guest, at his residence, to discuss with me a donation to the American-Arab Foundation and possibly collaborate with me in planning a major dinner for the Foreign Ambassador of Algeria (who was instrumental in the famous release of the 444 American hostages in Tehran, Iran).

Accordingly, my Executive Vice President drove me to the residence of the Ambassador of Algeria in a lovely part of Washington.

The Ambassador, dressed as neatly as any American diplomat, greeted me at the door, shook hands with me, and led me to the dining room, furnished with expensive rugs.

Then he invited me to sit next to him on a two-person couch, and I began discussing the goals of the Foundation and the generous support I had received from the Ambassador of Saudi Arabia last summer, and Qatar and Iraq.

At this point in the meeting, a servant came with an elaborate tray, smelling with the unmistakable aroma of strong coffee... and without asking me if I liked coffee or not, poured hot coffee into a large china cup and placed it before me. Then he repeated the same for the Ambassador who was sitting and smiling next to me.

Five minutes of our discussion passed, during which His Excellency, the Ambassador drank most of his coffee, but I did not even touch the cup before me.

A moment later, he said to me, "Mr. Rahawi, you forgot to drink your coffee. Let me get a fresh cup for you."

Immediately the servant appeared and replaced my cold coffee with another steaming cup.

As I looked at the second cup, I knew I was in trouble, because I could see that drinking his coffee was very important to my host, the Ambassador of Algeria to the United States of America. But then I was an active member of the Church of Jesus Christ of Latter-Day Saints, which teaches the importance of keeping the Word of Wisdom... including not drinking coffee.

The following few minutes were some of the most socially uncomfortable in my life.

The Ambassador stopped talking or listening to me. He was eyeing my cup of coffee to see when I would pick it up. When about five minutes passed, and my coffee cup was still untouched, he looked at me, his face glowing pink with indignation... and said to me as one deeply hurt, "Why are you rejecting my hospitality? Why don't you drink my coffee?"

I knew a storm was brewing, stronger than any coffee I ever drank before becoming a Mormon. But calmly and respectfully I said to him, while the two employees were standing by waiting, "Your Excellency, I assure you I am most grateful to be in your gracious home. I consider it a great honor for me to be your guest."

The Ambassador was looking at me, his face still glowing with indignation for ignoring his coffee.

Then I said, "Your Excellency, I used to love coffee and I drank 5-8 cups a day. But now I am a Mormon, and we Mormons don't drink coffee."

Instantly his face got redder, his eyes flashed with great surprise, and he said to me, "But your last name is Rahawi. I thought you were a Moslem American!"

I replied, calmly and respectfully, "Your Excellency, I was born in Iraq from Moslem parents, but as a citizen of the United States of America, I have the freedom to choose my faith... and I have chosen Jesus Christ. I became a Mormon Christian, and faithful Mormons don't drink coffee."

At that, the Ambassador got up, motioned (with his finger) for me to leave the house. I picked up my papers, put them in my briefcase, got up slowly and walked calmly out of the dining room into the entrance hall, and followed the Ambassador to the door.

As I was about to exit, I extended my right hand to shake his. He ignored my hand and instead said to me, "Please, don't come to the embassy anymore."

I replied to His Excellency, The Ambassador of Algeria, "I am sorry our meeting did not work out. But I thank you for inviting me to your beautiful home."

I then exited the front door, walked over to the foundation's Executive Vice President who had been waiting for me in his car the entire time I was at the Ambassador's residence.

After I sat next to him in the front seat, he looked at me anxiously and said, "That was a quick lunch. What happened?"

I then related what happened to the man who had been the third highest ranking CIA officer. After I finished, he smiled and said cheerfully, "In this world, ye shall have tribulation, be of good cheer."

Then he said, "How about lunch... without coffee?"

We both laughed and realized that the old saying, "You can't win them all" ... was true.

The following Sunday, I met with my Ward Bishop (in Mormon culture, the leader of the unit of the church to which I belong), and after a thorough discussion of the various aspects of the foundation and its circumstances and prospects, and my aspirations, he said to me,

"Young man, Steve A. Rahawi, go West to California. That is where you belong and that is where you will meet someone who will become your future wife."

Accordingly I resigned from my work as President and General Manager of The American-Arab Foundation, and delegated (with the approval of the Board of Directors in Salt Lake City) the remaining business of the foundation to the Executive Vice President, until the foundation ceases on its next license date.

Two days later, the Executive Vice President, his son, and I transferred to a pick-up many boxes containing foundation records, but mostly my personal effects to be placed at the Executive Vice President's large home until I established myself in California and asked him to ship my personal belongings to me.

I selected the following day, to be my last as a resident of Washington, D.C.... with undeniable nostalgia.

11

Good Bye Washington, D.C. Hello Los Angeles

The following morning, after I phoned many of my friends in and out of the church, and after I paid the full balance of my rent, leaving my room almost spotless (that is why the two hotel maids seemed to weep at my departure), I knelt on my knees in my room and offered a prayer of thanks for the privilege to have lived six months as a resident of our nation's capital, the beautiful Washington, D.C.

One hour later, I took my seat by the window, of a brand new Greyhound bus (bound for Los Angeles, California)... to cross the most beautiful country in the world, the United States of America... the country I love with all my heart and mind.

About 5:00 p.m. on July 29, 1981 I arrived at downtown Los Angeles, tired and hungry. But two hours later I was relaxing in the back yard of the beautiful home of my daughter, Susan. The house sat on a hillside in Malibu overlooking a magnificent view of the Pacific Ocean as it embraced the Southern California coast.

I stayed 40 days and nights, as a welcomed guest of my daughter Susan, my cute 20 month old grandson Matthew (Matt), and my darling little six month old grand daughter Elizabeth (Liz), and my 33 year old Jewish son-in-law.

Thus, at 54 and single, I became a newcomer to the Los Angeles area, and within a month, I learned that I was one of thousands of monthly newcomers who come to Los Angeles for Hollywood fame, a wild lifestyle, or wonderful sunshine, or the privilege to live in the most international city in the world, or all of these reasons plus a thousand of other possibilities.

During those 40 days at my daughter's home, I also had a wonderful time climbing up and down the neighboring landscape of the Malibu Hills with my study 21 month old grandson, Matt... who often led me to the neighborhood tennis court so he could see me serve the tennis ball right into the net, never above it, so he could run and return the ball to me for some more.

Then we would return home for me to

feed my little angelic granddaughter, Liz, in her high chair. Liz loved to hear me sing to her, "I am a child of God and he has sent me here... to parents kind and dear." Then I would feed her some more and re-sing, "I am a child of God..." until her brother Matt would get a little tired or maybe a little jealous of my obvious fun with his cute little sister, and would begin to pester her in her highchair, until I came to the rescue and lifted her up from her highchair in my cuddling arms, and then into her mother's or father's arms.

Interestingly, on the morning of my 40th day, after becoming a Southern California resident, I stood at the nearby Malibu Beach looking at the waves embracing the lovely beach.

As I stood there very relaxed, munching on a large and most delicious California grown peach, I felt a wonderful sense of peace. I knew that I had come to Southern California to live many, many long and faithful years.

The next Sunday I met with Bishop Tyler, the Bishop of the Pacific Palisades Ward, and he suggested that I consider serving in the Los Angeles Temple for a while.

Following Bishop Tyler's suggestion, and

armed with a letter of recommendation from him, I started serving daily (except Sundays and Mondays) at the Los Angeles Temple, that continued for 17 months. During this time (on September 9, 1981), I became a member of a ward located in a most beautiful chapel called "The Westwood Chapel", located at 10740 Ohio Avenue in Westwood, a peaceful community located in Western Los Angeles.

I love to attend church services on Sundays, almost every Sunday for the past 37 years.

In fact, I love to do all I can to serve in my assigned calling by church leaders whoever they are, regardless of age, color, financial or professional status.

I am currently serving about two hours weekly at the Los Angeles Temple, and about six hours weekly as a special representative of the Visitor Center.

At present I have an interesting assignment (until December 31, 2002), to keep our Westwood Chapel as a showcase for passersby as well as congregation members and visitors.

I am the Coordinator for keeping the Westwood Chapel in excellent order, neatness, cleanliness and safety.

I am assisted in this labor of love by three excellent volunteers: Paul B. Anderson, D.D.S., M.D., an oral and maxillofacial surgeon, Charles Forsher, a residential property manager, and Roberto Vasquez, an entrepreneur from New York. The four of us have become not only skilled in chapel maintenance tasks, but motivated by the cheerful spirit of Dr. Anderson, we have all become talented verbal comedians. And why not? We all live within three miles from Hollywood, the entertainment and fun capital of the world, as you, your spouse and your kids (especially the kids) know so well.

Yes, good bye Washington, D.C.... and Hello Los Angeles.

12

Double Career in L.A.: Selling Chambers/Writing Novels

After completing my 17 months service at the Los Angeles Temple, I started working as a Membership Representative for the Culver City Chamber of Commerce, then the Westwood Chamber of Commerce, and the Venice Chamber of Commerce... all located within the Western portion of the Los Angeles area. In this position, I managed to bring many hundreds of established, as well as newly formed, businesses into these three community-oriented business organizations.

While working as a Chamber of Commerce representative, I nurtured my keen interest in great Biblical stories, as the basis of successful docudramatic novels and/or great motion pictures, such as "The Ten Commandments" starring Charlton Heston.

Accordingly, I wrote my first docudramatic novel entitled "Abraham The Friend of God... The Spiritual Journey of a Great Prophet and the Three Women in His Life." A self-published edition of this novel has sold about 3,000 copies, yet I believe a national edition by a major publisher could sell 100 times more. I also believe this docudramatic novel has a potential to become a major motion picture... some day.

And again, my habitual interest in world events and international relations, particularly between the United States of America and the great people of the Russian Federation, prompted me to respond. After seeing a cold war movie bashing the Russians, instead of ending the movie on a positive note of goodwill, I resolved to write an American/Russian story of a different kind, a new type of American vs. Russian story. This story was to center around a terrific competition, dramatic and intense moments, humorous experiences and international romance, and to end in fantastic goodwill and wonderful discovery.

Thus, after eleven months of thinking, researching and talking to knowledgeable Americans and Russians, plus hundreds and hundreds of handwritten pages, I finally finished my second novel, and entitled it "No More Strangers: One American and Two Russians in a Helicopter Race Around the World".

Funny, I actually thought the world famous

Tom Cruise, could star as the very resilient American hero in my novel. Who knows? Maybe Tom Cruise may yet become so.

So far, my beloved novel "No More Strangers" and its older sister "Abraham" remain copyrighted with ISBN Numbers (ISBN 0-9652565-4-5 for Abraham The Friend of God; and ISBN 0-9652565-6-1 for No More Strangers).

And almost every night, I hear my charming novel "No More Strangers" whisper in my ear, "Steve, when are you going to wed me to a handsome and rich book publisher or Hollywood celebrity?" And every time I answer back, "Sweetheart, be patient. Your knight in shining armor shall knock with a bright gold wedding ring (meaning of course a qualified deal with a large cash advance)."

And now with this book I am preparing, "An American... Born in Iraq"... I have two babes on my neck and I need two knights in shining armor... unless the knight is a mighty prince who can handle both.

13

At 75... Happy, Healthy And Very Thankful

I am 75 years old, but most people tell me I look and act much younger. In fact, you may be surprised at the young women who eye me as I walk down the streets of Westwood looking happy, healthy and glad to be alive.

So what is my secret? Have I discovered the fountain of youth? No such thing. Youth pills? I take none. Perhaps secret plastic surgeries? Not one, I couldn't afford them if I wanted. Eight hours of beauty sleep every night? I am lucky if I get 6 1/2 hours.

I believe that my happiness, cheerfulness and gladness are almost entirely due to the fact that I am a thankful person. May I share with you why and how?

First of all... and above all else, I am very thankful to God who is my Heavenly Father. He has given me the privilege to live on the most beautiful planet... Mother Earth, which is second in beauty only to "Kolob", the governing planet... from where God the Eternal Father

(Elohim) rules the universe with wonderful perfection.

I consider it a great honor to share our magnificent and very productive Earth with only about 6 Billion human beings, about one billion dogs, and about a billion cats, and perhaps 300 million horses. And what about the 20 billion beautiful trees and the trillion most colorful flowers on a spring day in the Northern Hemisphere?

And what about the two trillion fishes of unbelievable varieties and shapes? So how can I but be very thankful and glad for all these creations of God Almighty?

(Important Note: Please forgive me if I did not mention your favorite animal, plant or bird or insect or fish by name. There must be at least trillions and trillions of living things... belonging to our Earth. It is mind boggling to think how intelligent and creative God is.

Second of all... I am indeed very thankful to know that Jesus Christ was resurrected the Third Day, after He was crucified... and that He did ascend to heaven to live with God forever... and that he is my Savior and Deliverer from my sins (for I am only a man, and a weak one at that in many ways). So every time I partake of the Sacrament of Bread and

Water on Sundays, if I am sincere in asking forgiveness of my sins of the past week... He (Jesus Christ) does become my advocate with our Heavenly Father, and they both forgive my sins... and command me (lovingly) to repent.

Believe me ladies and gentlemen, this weekly repentance and forgiveness is a wonderful comfort to me. It does give me renewed bounce and good cheer.

Third of all... I am thankful for all the Holy Scriptures, especially the Holy Bible and the Book of Mormon... because both of them teach me how to serve and love my family members and my friends and neighbors... and all my fellow human beings, all of which give me joy, confidence, renewed energy and vitality and sincere, friendly and happy smiles.

Fourth of all... I am very thankful to my parents who lived and died in Iraq.

They were illiterate and unlearned in modern philosophies about raising children, but they did love me and did miss me terribly. Neither of them ever saw me again after I left Mosul to come to America.

My heart turned to them, wonderfully, when I learned that my first given name "Ahmad" was the last word my father said when he died at the age of 50, due to excessive smoking.

This parental love I know, coupled with my complete faith that I will meet and know my parents again in the next life after death, gives me peace of heart and mind... which does reflect in my well being emotionally and physically.

Fifth of all...I am thankful for each of my teachers, at elementary school, junior high, high school, A.U.B. in Beirut, and the University of Denver.

I will ever be grateful for that teacher in Mosul, who slapped my face so hard I landed on the floor when I was eleven years old. He taught me a great lesson in obedience to law and authority.

I am equally thankful to all those who taught me in the business world and at church.

Without my caring teachers, I would have had a terrible and destructive character, and perhaps I would have been dead or deformed a long time ago.

Sixth of all... I am thankful to each of my beautiful daughters: Susan, Patricia and Sonja. Each is unique; each is worthy of my gratitude to God. I love each of them, and I believe each of them loves me too.

I am also thankful for my son, Dan Joseph, who died as a small infant. I have faith that I will continue as his earthly father in the Millennium. Then I will play with him, teach him, and see him grow up to adulthood.

I am thankful for my 23 year old grandson, Matt, and my 21 year old granddaughter, Liz. They are part of my prayer because I love them and I have great hopes for them and through them. I don't act as an old Grandad with either of them, do I Matt and Liz?

Seventh of all... I am thankful to God Almighty and to my doctor, Abraham Waks, and to Ralph's grocery stores... for my healthy diet with hardly any meat, lots of fruit and vegetables (especially tomatoes), wheat bread and cereals, and good old peanut butter.

I must now mention my lifelong love for walking, brisk and joyful walking, miles every day and at least two miles on Sundays. I can add to that my daily morning limbering exercises, including my eyes, neck and hands.

This is not bragging, but the truth is I have never (since that terrible cigarette when I was 16) smoked another cigarette; And, I have never had a drop of alcohol, coffee or tea for the past 37 years.

The result of this combination of diet and exercise is very good. I have a lot of vitality, stamina and freedom from dependence on the never-ending stream of health related information and inducements.

Please feel free to laugh or smile, but the truth is that since I was delivered by that midwife in Mosul until now, I have been a patient in a hospital only twice; once for several days in a hospital in Baghdad for a gland operation when I was about five...and for two hours observation in a Stillwater, Oklahoma hospital for suspected food poisoning when I was eating, unthoughtfully, all kinds of food at age 31.

Eighth of all... I am thankful for my friends: Oscar winning director Kieth Merrill, international music composer Merrill Jenson, and photography director Reed Smooth... for encouraging me to write my two novels, "Abraham The Friend of God" and "No More Strangers" in a form that could be easily adapted into screenplays for appealing feature films.

I am particularly thankful for my friends: Dr. Paul Anderson, UCLA Retired Professor Arthur Wallace, Dale Wagstaff, Bishop Bragg, actor model David Else, and my computer expert, Chris... for encouraging me to begin and continue writing "An American... Born in Iraq".

Ninth of all... I am thankful to be a citizen of the United States, a resident of Los Angeles, California, and a Democrat at times, then a Republican at times... but a lover of America always.

Tenth of all... I am thankful for every day and each night, for the sunshine, for the dark and the fluffy white clouds, for the rain and fog, for the fresh air that fills my lungs, and for the beauty of the Earth and the beauty of the skies wherever I am.

Even though I never had a dog or cat as a pet, yet as I pass by my neighbors' cats and dogs... and look with understanding heart, I become thankful too for the sweet soft meowing cats, and the friendly dogs wiggling their tails with joy for a loving touch.

Last but dearest to my dreams, I am thankful for the beautiful woman whom God shall help me date, then marry in his holy temple, to become my wife, my sweetheart, my companion and my dependable supporter and friend.

No wonder at 75... I am happy, healthy, and very thankful.

14

Lessons I learned from My Two Marriages

I made many mistakes in my two marriages. As I look back realistically, I can honestly state that each of my two former wives had her good qualities. I am grateful to each, for bearing two beautiful children, who became her children and mine. I ask God's blessings upon each of them in her righteous labors and desires. I thank each for every good she added to my life, and ask their forgiveness and my children's forgiveness for my errors of the past, about 90% of which were unintentional, due to life's pressures coupled with a lack of wisdom.

I am sorry I could not love my second wife's children from her former marriage, as my own.

And now I wish to share my sincere thoughts with you, on how to plan and live a lasting marriage. My suggestions are intended for men, but women will benefit as well.

1. Marry a friend. Some physical at-

traction is essential, but sincere, mutual and happy friendship before marriage is a most reliable foundation and pillar for marriage.

2. Don't rush into making or accepting a marriage proposal. Take at least a month to realistically consider the pros and cons of your relationship and circumstances, before you become engaged or married.

3. Be cheerful, flexible and humorous daily. Accept the challenges which any marriage encounters. Make compromises and express thanks to your spouse and to each of your children, at least once a day.

4. Take time with your spouse and your children, to read, every morning or evening, at least for five minutes in the Holy Bible or the Book of Mormon. End each scripture reading with a family prayer offered by you or your spouse or one of your children. Express thanks to God for your family unit and ask his continued blessings. The father in the family decides who offers the prayer, with kindness and love, not as a stern boss.

5. Money is important. Professional, business or charity work is important. But marital and family happiness is much more important, a thousand times more important. Your spouse is indeed more important to you

than any other person in the world. Plan and act accordingly every day, every week, every month, and everywhere.

6. Love of God, love of family, love of community and one's country... and respect and care and love for our neighbors... are true commandments from God to all mankind. Doing so will surely give a person and spouse greater balance and happiness at home and at work... by day and by night.

7. Sex outside marriage is poison; as part of marriage sex is wonderful. Entice your spouse, by glance, touch or words, to desire sex with you. Take a vacation of fun and sex, with your spouse only, at least one or two nights four times a year. Be sure, absolutely sure, that you give your spouse at least once a week arousing sexual intercourse, coupled with exciting words of love and gratitude. You can do it. If you don't know how or can't, ask God the wisest of all to help you do so. He will, because he wants you and your spouse to be contented and loyal to each other... from the first day of marriage until death separates you.

Be sure that you don't tell anyone else about your sex life with your spouse. It is sacred and secret and must so remain. Finally, avoid pornography. You don't need it. Concentrate on the talents of each other and the surprising thrills with each other.

15

My Vision of U.S.-Iraq Relations

We Americans are the most forgiving nation on earth. We forgave Japan and Germany after we conquered both in World War II. May we also forgive and extend a helping hand to Iraq and its peoples of all faiths and racial groupings... when Iraq is no longer a threat.

I have a vision of Iraq as the best friend to America in the Middle East, like Israel, with economic collaboration for the benefit of both nations: trading the high quality Iraqi oil in exchange for America's know-how in petrochemical projects and agricultural development. Then, Iraqi dates (not the opposite sex kind, but the deliciously edible kind) will be welcomed by American housewives and a famous nice First Lady called Laura Bush. This is my vision. May it come to pass within three years from September 11, 2008.

And when religious and political freedoms are established in Iraq, to an acceptable degree

like they are in Russia now, Iraq shall prove
to be the brightest star in the roster of Arabic
speaking nations.

16

Salute to Freedom
Salute to America

And now... as I write the 16th chapter of this book "An American... Born in Iraq", I humbly express my everlasting gratitude to God Almighty who is the author of liberty and all true freedoms.

Oh precious freedoms: Freedom of Choice, Freedom of Belief, Freedom of Worship, Freedom of Speech, Freedom of the Press, Freedom of Assembly, Freedom as manifested by the majority vote... without fear or oppression.

I support and defend all these freedoms and all other freedoms as proclaimed in the greatest document of human liberty and justice: The Constitution of the United States of America.

May the bells of these freedoms continue to ring, loud and clear, in the U.S.A.... soon in Iraq... and more and more in all the world.

This is my belief, my hope, my pleading... my Salute to Freedom everywhere... my Salute to America, the country which I have loved very much... since I was a youth in Mosul, Iraq.

May all who live in the Land of the Free and the Home of the Brave, unitedly and often, place our right hands over our hearts and say aloud,

"I pledge allegiance to the Flag

of the United States of America,

and to the republic for which it stands,

one nation under God, indivisible,

with Liberty and Justice for all."

17

My Autobiography in Pictures

My Father, Abdul-Aziz Rahawi, at age 47.
Picture was taken on February 16, 1945 in Mosul, Iraq.

My Mother, Hayat Killah Rahawi, at age 70.
Picture was taken in 1968 in Baghdad, Iraq.

That's me, in 1939, at age 13 in Mosul, Iraq.
Good looking, but thoughtful too, don't you think?

My Father, far right, with two of his closest friends:
The City Judge and the City Tax Collector,
in his office in 1943 in Mosul, Iraq.

ABOVE: My high school (for selected male students)
in Baghdad, Iraq, in September 1943.

BELOW: My high school graduation class picture,
in June 1944. I am 9th from the right in the second row.

My Half-sister Adeeba in Mosul, Iraq, at 16 in 1946, pictured in our family's fruit and vegetable garden. She was one in only eight known female tennis players in Mosul.

ABOVE: My dormitory in September 1946, at A.U.B.
(The American University in Beirut, Lebanon)

BELOW: View of Beirut, Lebanon in September 1946
… and the hills overlooking the Mediterranean Sea.

ABOVE: Me (smiling) and Egyptian Dr. Ibraheem, February 1947 on the deck of the passenger ship "Al Sudan", the third day of our voyage from Alexandria to New York.

BELOW: A view of the famous Rock of Gibraltar which I photographed from the wobbly deck of our ship.

Ahmad Rahawi

"These impressions of the United
States have been received within
the past 10 days by Ahmad Rahawi, native of Baghdad, Iraq,
who is in Denver to become a student at the University of Denver."

Photograph and excerpt from an article of the
March 5, 1947 issue of The Rocky Mountain News
in Denver, Colorado.

ABOVE: That is not an Eskimo. That is me, Ahmad Tobogganing in February 1948 in hills West of Denver.

BELOW: By April 1948, I was the snow man from Iraq, enjoying my pals at the University of Denver.

This is me in December 1950 as a full-time University of
Denver student and part-time insurance agent.

* * * * * * * * * * * * * * *

STEVE A. RAHAWI

*Steve Rahawi, a native son
of* Iraq, *came to this
country about three years
ago. Since that time, he
has mastered our language,
and made A grades at the
University of Denver. He
started with the World last
June and has given the "top
honor" boys a run to keep up
with him. He carries a full
schedule in college and
writes insurance on the side.
He says "hard work" and
"never say die" are the
pass words to successful
production.*

As a university graduate, a naturalized citizen of the
United States of America, a successful insurance general agent, a married man and a father of two cute little
girls
(Susan and Patricia), the State of Kansas decided
to give me a hearty welcome... and I loved it.

SUSAN

PATRICIA   SONJA

My three beautiful daughters, all born in the U.S.A....
all are different and precious.

My brother Thamir at 36 in Baghdad with his children.

Here I go again, relaxing after completing my
second novel entitled "No More Strangers".

In memory of my son, Dan Joseph, who died when 89 days old... without any picture taken of him.

I am comforted by my Faith, that my son, Dan Joseph... as well as all children in all the world, who died and who will die, before the age of eight years... are saved in the life after death, and will enjoy Eternal Peace... through Jesus Christ, the Prince of Peace.

ABOVE: My first born daughter, Susan, as a teenager.

BELOW: My second born daughter, Patricia
as a teenager.

My third born daughter, Sonja, just loves to ride horses;
as a child, at 28 and probably always.

My daughter, Susan and her son, my Grandson, Matt.

ABOVE: My Grandson, Matt, Malibu Junior High School,
Los Angeles, California

BELOW: My Granddaughter, Liz, Malibu Junior High
School, Los Angeles, California

NOT SO TIGHT GRANDPA! Horsing around with
my two Grandchildren. In the middle is their cousin.

My daughter Susan (left), a Real Estate Agent

My daughter, Patricia (right), an Art Dealer

My Third Daughter Sonja in front of me.
My Step_children Mark & Vicki on my sides.

Above: With my daughter Susan in Denver, Colorado

Below: With my daughter Patricia in Denver, Colorado

188

Near Malibu, California,
my daughter Susan on my right, my daughter Patricia on my
left, and the jealous Pacific Ocean, screaming behind us.

My Granddaughter Liz and I becoming Pals
in her home in Malibu, California...
home of the Stars and wonderful Sunsets.

My daughter, Sonja and I in Susan's back yard in Malibu,
I at 71 and she at 27. Prior to this picture, Sonja and I had
not seen each other for 20 long, long years.

Above: With my second Grandson "Dillon"...
minutes after waking up from a rare afternoon nap.

Below: Dillon, wearing two rubber
fingers, announces he is four years old.